A MINISTRY OF CARE

Promoting Health in Your Faith Community

Cynthia A. Russell, PhD, RN, FAAN, PCC, CBCC, NBC-HWC

Kristen L. Mauk, PhD, DNP, RN, CRRN, GCNS-BC, GNP-BC, ACHPN, FAAN

THE FOUNDRY

PUBLISHING

Cover design: Merit Alcala
Interior design: Sharon Page

Library of Congress Cataloging-in-Publication Data
Names: Russell, Cynthia A., 1956- author.
Title: A ministry of care : promoting health in your faith community / Cynthia A.
    Russell, PhD, RN, FAAN, PCC, CBCC, NBC-HWC, Kristen L. Mauk, PhD, DNP,
    RN, CRRN, GCNS-BC, GNP-BC, ACHPN, FAAN.
Description: Kansas City, MO : Foundry Publishing, 2019. | Includes bibliographical
    references.
Identifiers: LCCN 2018043566 | ISBN 9780834137622 (pbk.)
Subjects: LCSH: Church work with the sick. | Healing—Religious aspects—
    Christianity. | Medical care—Religious aspects—Christianity.
Classification: LCC BV4460 .R87 2019 | DDC 259/.4—dc23
LC record available at https://lccn.loc.gov/2018043566

The internet addresses, email addresses, and phone numbers in this book are accurate at the time of publication. They are provided as a resource. The Foundry Publishing does not endorse them or vouch for their content or permanence.

CONTENTS

PART ONE

Becoming Health Aware

1

WHY ADDRESS HEALTH ISSUES?

"I have come that they may have life,
and have it to the full."
—John 10:10b

"Lord we pray for healing and peace for the frail and the sick. We pray for those hurting in body, mind, and spirit. Especially we pray for John after his heart attack; for Jenny's aunt Thelma following the amputation of her foot; for Anne with her diagnosis of breast cancer; for Alex as he transitions to the memory care center; for Shalina as she struggles with depression and thoughts of self-harm; and for all those unnamed who are dealing with illness and pain."

Have you or has someone you know prayed a prayer similar to this one? Illness—and its impact on our lives—is never far from our thoughts and actions as we worship together. This consciousness is not surprising when we take into account that one in two Americans suffers from a chronic disease such as hypertension, coronary heart disease, stroke, diabetes, cancer, arthritis, hepatitis, weak or failing kidneys, asthma, or chronic obstructive pulmonary disease (COPD).[1] As you look down the pew, imagine that one in two people (which, in a pew seating ten, would be five) is living with a serious health condition. Little wonder our prayer lists for health and restoration grow longer every week.

What would happen if, in our places of faith, we took aim at embracing health with the goal of reversing the downward spiral of disease? How many lives would be changed? While well grounded in inspiring spiritual well-being, local churches are ideally positioned to facilitate a renewed commitment to overall health and wellness in their members' lives and in the lives of the many people whom they reach in their communities.

Historically, the church has been a place for both physical and spiritual health. Jesus spent the majority of his earthly ministry performing many miracles, including healing the blind, the lame, and the sick, and even raising people from the dead. Although physical healing is the accompanying outcome of some of these stories, spiritual healing usually precedes it in the form of forgiveness, cleansing, or freedom. As Matthew 9:35 records, "Jesus went through all the towns and villages, teaching in their synagogues, proclaiming the good news of the kingdom and healing every disease and sickness." In the early Christian church, the disciples of Christ continued this tradition of ministering to the sick and diseased. In later years, many Catholic and Protestant nursing orders were formed to care for the sick. Now, as then, many congregations continue to provide care for the sick and poor.

Today, churches have an opportunity to focus on promoting health and the *prevention* of disease. Advancements in science and the ease of access to use this knowledge to promote health create a powerful path to lifestyle change. Small changes in food choices, physical activity, and stress management can add up to significant improvements in one's health and sense of well-being. Increasing the knowledge of individuals in relation to key health concerns and medical management is a means to affect the health of the congregation. Add to this the social support of the church family and the ability to expand in relationship to God, others, and oneself, and the church, through its members, has all the key elements to promote a healthy life.

This book is about reclaiming Christ's ministry in its fullness to include a focus on all dimensions of the human experience: mind, body, and spirit. Part 1 provides the context for building a congregational awareness of how healthy people can better serve God, their families, and their communities. Part 2 offers how-to steps with practical information to address common health concerns and issues, along with health-promotion activities for church members and the larger community. Part 3 expands the reach of the congregation with a focus on current healthcare trends and ways to enhance and maintain a health-ministry team.

 **Are You Health Aware?**

Think about the past month in the life of your church. What health issues have impacted the members of your church community? How have these issues affected the individual, the family, the congregation, and the community at large?

What is your congregation currently doing to support parishioners in attaining and maintaining healthy lives?

How did Christ and his disciples promote the health of individuals? Consider the following scriptures:

- Matthew 25:35–40

- Mark 2:1–12

- Mark 2:17

- John 4

- John 10:10

- Acts 5:12–16

- James 5:14–16

 Next Steps

Right now we can:

Within three months, we will:

Our end-of-year goal is:

2

BIRTH TO ADVANCED AGE

"For we were born only yesterday and know nothing,
and our days on earth are but a shadow."
—Job 8:9

As you enter the sanctuary before the service begins, your eyes scan the congregation. You look to the left and notice Jenny and Mike, a young couple filled with expectation as they await the birth of their first child. Just ahead of them, John sits with his head bowed in prayerful reflection. You remember the many years that Sarah joined him in that very pew. They had been married nearly fifty years when Sarah died of lung cancer last year. Suddenly, your eyes dart in the opposite direction, following the sound of a joyful shriek exploding from two-year-old Tina, whose older brother is making silly faces. Their adolescent sister, Lorna, is mortified, while their parents exchange knowing glances. As the service starts, you whisper a word of blessing over these and all members of the congregation, thankful for the richness of your church community.

As an elder of the church, a lay leader, a minister, priest, rabbi, or as any member of the congregation who understands the importance of health, you know that in order to promote good health within the congregation, you must first understand basic human development. This chapter explores some of the major development milestones from conception to late adulthood, providing a snapshot of the physical, cognitive, and psychosocial development that typically occurs at each of life's stages. With a special focus on topics of particular relevance to the health ministry within your church, you will be able to assess the various needs in your congregation and consider ways to meet them. A table at the end of the chapter summarizes key considerations for each stage.

Prenatal to Birth

The miracle of birth begins when a sperm and an egg combine. From this point on the cells continue to divide with natural points of reference including the embryo (two to eight weeks) and the fetus (two months to birth). Though miraculously complex, all of the biological information required for development of the human body is present at conception. During the next thirty-eight weeks or so, growth and development of the unborn baby occurs at an amazing rate. The mother's nutritional state, age, drug and alcohol intake, health status, physical activity, stress levels, and exposure to environmental hazards all affect the prenatal environment of the fetus. It is significant that most birth defects and miscarriages occur in the first three months of pregnancy. Up to 20 percent of all pregnancies end in miscarriage, often without the woman's knowledge. The process of labor and delivery typically lasts fourteen to twenty-six hours, though this timing can be much shorter or much longer. Contractions are often painful, usually increasing in frequency and duration as labor progresses. Following the birth of the baby, the mother delivers the afterbirth, or placenta.

Childbirth classes can help increase the parents' comfort level with the delivery process, and this is one area where your church ministry can assist. Consider opening your facility for birthing classes where women and their support partners can experience the embrace of the congregation as they prepare for the birth of their babies.

It is significant to note that approximately 32 percent of babies born in the United States are delivered by cesarean section (the surgical removal of the baby from the mother's uterus).[1] This surgical procedure can increase the time needed to recover from the birth experience.

Though most babies are born healthy, some are born too soon or are too small. An infant is considered premature when born before the completion of thirty-seven weeks of gestation. A low-birth-weight infant weighs under five pounds, eight ounces, while infants considered very low-birth-weight weigh under three pounds, three ounces. Many factors contribute to the underweight birth of infants. Use the list below and consider what steps your congregation could take to mitigate these factors in the lives of mothers in your community:

- Mother is under 17 or over 40 years of age
- Mother lives in poverty
- Mother has a low level of education
- Mother is single
- Mother smokes
- Mother practices poor nutritional habits
- Mother uses drugs or alcohol during pregnancy
- Mother has already had multiple pregnancies
- Mother has had inadequate or no prenatal care
- Mother suffers from other health conditions

Pregnancy is a time of transition, whether it is a long-awaited event or an unintended surprise. You can help with this transition by promoting opportunities for pregnant women or couples to discuss their hopes and fears associated with pregnancy, birth, and childrearing. If the pregnancy is not welcome, then a woman or couple may seek counsel and guidance.

Celebrating new birth is an obvious and easy way for the church to support families. However, new and hopeful parents may encounter significant challenges that open the door for ministry opportunities.

Infertility

Infertility is the inability to conceive a child despite trying for one year. The experience of infertility often results in pain, frustration, and isolation. A couple dealing with infertility may be tempted to blame God despite the fact that infertility is fairly common. Finding ways to support these couples can be as simple as connecting them with someone who has experienced what they're going through or as complex as hosting and/or facilitating a support group as an outreach into the community.

The couple may want to seek guidance from their church community concerning the options the medical community may offer, and it may help for your church to have a basic understanding of what those options are. These options can include assisted reproductive technologies (ART) and in-vitro fertilization (IVF) including the implantation of multiple embryos, the use of donor eggs, or the disposition of frozen embryos. Infertility can put great stress on a couple, so having the support of a church community is extremely important.

Miscarriage and Infant Death

Loss of pregnancy through miscarriage, stillbirth, or the death of a newborn is an emotionally devastating experience that requires much support. Grief is a natural reaction, and parents can feel isolated when the larger community does not recognize the extent of their loss. Churches can play an important role in supporting parents who have experienced this kind of loss through the grieving process and helping them adjust to their new reality. Churches can do this by offering spiritual guidance and promoting compassion in the congregational community.

Postpartum Depression

Many people think that the days following a baby's birth are, or should be, extremely happy for new parents. And often times they are, but even the most well-adjusted parent may sometimes feel down during this period. A new mother, in particular, has to respond to rapid changes in her body, including hormone levels, physical exhaustion, and unaccustomed demands like breastfeeding and disrupted sleep patterns. For most women, this emotional disruption is short-lived.

Studies suggest that between 10 to 14 percent of women who have given birth experience a condition known as postpartum depression (PPD). PPD is a serious condition that can result in mothers attempting to hurt themselves, their infants, and/or their other children. Be attentive to signs of possible PPD and act as a resource for mothers to get professional help when that is required.

Symptoms of PPD may include feelings of sadness and/or hopelessness, frequent crying, anxiety, irritability, issues with sleep (too much or too little), loss of interest in previously pleasurable activities, difficulty concentrating, inability to make decisions, unusual anger or rage, physical pain (muscle aches, headaches), weight changes, withdrawal from others, inability to bond with the baby, doubts of ability to care for the baby, and thoughts of harming the baby. Should these or similar symptoms present, assist the new mother in seeking professional help from her obstetrician or primary care provider.

Multiple Births

Pregnancies involving multiple births (twins, triplets, etc.) can be very stressful for a couple. Multiple births can be difficult to carry to term, often producing premature babies with low birth weight. Members of the church can provide spiritual and practical support for the couple so that they can face the challenges of high-risk births. Some examples of support might include creating a family care circle to support the family before and after the babies are born. The church community might assist by providing child-care for other siblings, helping with household chores, dropping off grocery staples from the store, preparing easy-to-cook meals, celebrating positive developments, and offering prayers and support during challenging times.

Birth Defects and Other Diagnoses

When a newborn has a birth defect or other serious health condition, parents are certain to feel threatened by the situation. Already exhausted from the birthing experience, their idea of the perfect child is shattered, and the care of their infant is complicated. A church community's role in helping guide them through the grief process and providing spiritual comfort will be invaluable. A church community may be able to assist the family in navigating through the often confusing medical environment, finding ways to pay for expensive care for their infant, and supporting other children in the family, should they exist. If older siblings do exist, remember to pay special attention to them. The younger they are, the easier it is for them to feel neglected when a new sibling is receiving so much attention. Members of the church community can make it their mission to minister to this family by spending time specifically with older siblings, letting them know they are special children of God and that they are loved.

Infancy and Toddlerhood: Birth to 3 Years

The time from birth to three years of age is an explosive period of growth and development. To put it into perspective, the infant's birth weight typically triples by the first birthday, and developmentally, the little bundle in one's arms evolves to walking and talking. The list below provides a brief summary that highlights some of these miraculous changes:

- Newborns sleep up to 17 hours per day initially. This decreases over time.

- Newborns function with primitive reflexes that evolve into gross and fine motor skills. Typically, babies can grasp a rattle at 4 months, roll over at 5 months, sit without support at 7 months, and stand with support at 9 months.
- Babies say their first words by 1 year, though by 9 months they begin to understand some words.
- 90 percent of babies can walk by 15 months.
- At 24 months, most children begin to run and jump in place and can kick and throw a ball.
- At age 2, most children have a vocabulary of about 100 words and are putting together simple sentences.
- At 3 years, most children are toilet trained.
- Emotions evolve in complexity over time from distress and interest to anger, joy, fear, sadness, and more.
- Temperaments vary. Where some children are easygoing, happy, and quick to adapt to change, others may be harder to please, irritable, more expressive of extreme emotions, and slow to adapt to change.

How might these general developmental milestones come into play within a church family? First-time parents might wonder about how their baby is developing in comparison to other children. It is important to reinforce that each child is unique and that these milestones provide general guidelines for expected behavior but that they aren't set in stone. A child developing at a slower or faster rate than these guidelines set is not necessarily cause for concern. Encourage parents to discuss any concerns regarding their individual child's development with a pediatrician. Church nursery volunteers should be aware of basic developmental stages so they can care for children while creating a safe and supportive environment.

The process of becoming part of a family is a major developmental feature for a young child. This process is referred to as attachment—the bond between the caregiver and the infant. According to psychologist Erik Erikson, the period from infancy to 18 months is the time when infants deal with basic trust versus basic mistrust.[2] At this time, the infant develops a sense of the world as a good and safe place (trust). When a child determines that his or her world is not a safe place, mistrust occurs. Erikson's second stage, called "autonomy versus shame and doubt," happens between ages 1 and 3.[3] Here the child becomes more independent from the parents, doing such things as walking, exploring, and deciding what to eat. Success here breeds more independence or autonomy, while the child who experiences parental criticism or overprotection is at risk of feeling doubt and shame.

How can the congregation support parents of infants and toddlers?

- **Consider offering parenting classes and parenting support groups.** Most parents welcome opportunities to compare notes and share the adventures and misadventures of parenting.
- **Schedule a new parent tour of or visit to the nursery.** This provides the parents with the opportunity to see the facility, meet the volunteers, and become acquainted with policies and procedures.
- **Provide age-appropriate milestone index cards when the child uses the church nursery.** Useful information can be provided along with messages of God's love and support from the congregation.
- **Host age-specific workshops that tap into community experts.** Local colleges and community centers have experts who love to share their knowledge.
- **Consider providing daycare services so that working parents have a quality childcare option.** Most parents work outside the home, so knowing that their child is in a caring, faith-based environment can make this particular parental challenge a little easier.
- **Create a closed online group where parents can bring their questions and share the highs and lows of parent-**

ing. Today, social media offers an alternative to leaving the home and provides an open space for dialogue and support.

Early Childhood: Ages 3 to 6 Years

Physical growth continues at a quick pace, though it is slower than in infancy. Children at these ages are able to engage in many activities because of the progress made in motor development. They are able to run, skip, jump, hop, and throw balls in early childhood. With advancement of fine motor skills, they can draw pictures with crayons or markers, button their shirts, and tie their shoes.

The advances young children make in cognitive development also continue at a rapid rate. During early childhood, children use symbols, meaning they think about something without needing it in front of them. The ability to organize or classify objects begins during these years. Children understand numbers and learn to count. The many "why" questions that three- to six-year-olds ask are evidence of developing cause-and-effect thinking. Parents and others need to remember, however, that the thinking of the young child is still evolving and is still not logical. In early childhood, language skills continue to progress with an increase in vocabulary and more application of grammar and syntax. Parents with questions about delays in their child's language development should discuss their concerns with a healthcare provider.

According to Erikson, resolving the tensions between initiative and guilt is the task of early childhood.[4] Initiative refers to the child's efforts to engage in purposeful activities, while guilt can occur as a result of experiencing disapproval from others for these activities. Play, and especially imaginative play, is an important way for children to develop social and cognitive skills. Children learn about gender roles by modeling the behaviors of the culture and start to align themselves with friends of the same sex. The self-concept, or how one views one's own self, begins to evolve.

How can the congregation support parents with children in early childhood?

- **Offer parenting classes and parenting support groups.**
  Important topics include child safety and preventing accidents, addressing sleep disturbances, bed-wetting, and
  discipline.
- **Host health-promotion workshops for young children.**
  Children at this age love learning about their bodies. Consider a "glow germ" program on hand-washing that shows
  how germs remain after ineffective hand-washing. Other
  topics, from brushing teeth to what to eat, can significantly
  impact young minds.
- **Target a closed online group for parents of three- to six-
  year-olds.** The challenges of parenting evolve as children
  mature. This congregation-sponsored social media provides
  a safe haven to ask questions and find support.
- **Start a Mothers of Preschoolers (MOPs) group.** MOPs
  is a church-hosted program that allows mothers to gather
  regularly and share the joys and frustrations of motherhood
  in a safe, relaxing environment. To find out more, go to
  mops.org.

Middle and Late Childhood: Ages 6 to 12 Years

This is quite a span of ages that basically relates to the grade-
school-age child. The physical growth of children is slower during
this period even as fine and gross motor skills and mental ability
expand at a tremendous pace. Children become more coordinated,
faster, and stronger during this time period. Sports programs can
offer wonderful opportunities for children to learn to compete,
develop team-building skills, enhance self-esteem, work out regularly, and promote physical health. However, increased competition and pressure from parents and coaches can cause children
to experience stress in relation to their activities. The pressure to
achieve can be extreme and must be managed carefully.

Memory, language skills, and communication improve significantly during middle and late childhood. Children learn to

think logically because they can consider multiple factors at once. Problem-solving skills evolve, as does the ability to take on more of a worldview that sees another's point of view. The ability to work with numbers and to recognize individual things in relation to their classes continues to develop.

According to developmental psychologist Jean Piaget, young children are guided by fixed and rigid rules.[5] As children mature into middle and late childhood, they begin to have a broader understanding of right and wrong that is characterized by flexibility. For the church, this stage provides a critical period when biblical stories and current events can be explored in the context of right and wrong in order to help shape moral development.

Erikson suggests that the task of middle childhood is "industry versus inferiority."[6] The child develops a sense of competence when they are able to master skills and finish tasks. If a child struggles in this area, they are at risk of feeling inferior to peers and others.

How can the congregation support parents and children in middle and late childhood?

- **Establish child-friendly and family-friendly sports programs.** Help children learn how to be good winners and losers. Set up a league with other faith-based groups to create an opportunity to embrace diversity. Upward Sports (upward.org) offers one model. This is also a great way to increase exercise in the child's daily routine.

- **Parenting classes and parenting support groups.** Information related to issues that surface for children in school, such as attention deficit disorders, learning disabilities, and depression can be very helpful. Be sensitive to create an inclusive environment that serves the members of your congregation and their children.

- **Host health-promotion workshops for families with older children.** Many children are already obese by the middle childhood years. Nutrition and cooking classes can be fun and help trim the waistline. Low-calorie and low-sugar foods can make a big difference.

Adolescence: 13 to 18 Years

Adolescence is the transitional stage between childhood and adulthood. Adolescence is most commonly recognized as a period of physical change but may also involve cognitive, emotional, and social upheaval. Adolescence starts with the onset of puberty, or the beginning of sexual maturity and the biological ability to reproduce. For many Americans, adolescence begins well before the age of thirteen, perhaps as early as age seven. Adolescence may continue for some young people into their early twenties.

Rapid growth in weight and height occurs with the onset of puberty as well as muscular and skeletal development. Along with sexual maturity, body proportions and form change. Young people begin to take on the body shapes of the adults they will become. Be prepared for adolescents in your congregation to mature at different rates.

In addition to the physical changes, adolescents experience mental changes as well. This is a time when abstract thinking further evolves, along with hypothetical-deductive reasoning. Closely related to these new cognitive abilities is moral development. As early as age thirteen, some teens can make judgments related to basic principles of fairness and justice.

The basic question for adolescents, according to Erikson, is "Who am I?"[7] Young people work toward understanding themselves in terms of occupation, values they will live by, and sexual identity. This long-term process involves experimentation and exploration that can continue well into their twenties and beyond.

Many teenagers become sexually active, putting themselves at risk for sexually transmitted diseases, pregnancy, and emotional trauma. While some churches may be able to handle these sensitive issues, it is important that youth ministers and other church leaders know where to find support in the community to assist teens and their families.

How can the congregation support parents and teens?

- **Host concurrent but separate classes for teenagers and parents.** Distinct groups create a more comfortable space to share experiences, concerns, and fears with their peers. Important subjects include the use of drugs and alcohol, high-risk behaviors, sexual activity, pregnancy, suicide, and eating disorders. Consider inviting community experts to present to the groups.

- **Maintain a list of qualified health professionals in the community to support physical and emotional issues of teens and their families.** When parents or teens (or both) come looking for resources, churches should be ready to equip them beyond pastoral counseling and guidance.

Early Adulthood: 19 to 39 Years

Young adults, their growth complete, are typically at their peak physical level of health with an emphasis on endurance and strength. According to the Centers for Disease Control and Prevention (CDC), the leading causes of death for 25- to 34-year-olds are accidents, suicide, and homicide, while those ages 35 to 44 die from accidents, malignancy, and heart disease in that order.[8]

As young adults finish their education, many secure work in their chosen profession and move out of their parents' homes. According to Erikson, the young adult makes the choice between intimacy and isolation.[9] Intimacy means the ability to commit to a close, personal relationship. As Erikson sees it, falling in love and having children are evidence of successful completion of this stage. For Erikson, those who are afraid or unable to commit to a relationship will be isolated and self-absorbed.

How can the congregation support young adults?

- **Host a series of seminars about relationships.** Whether young adults are already partnered or are still single, discussions about healthy communication, self-awareness, and lasting relationships facilitate growth for evolving adults.

- **Encourage young adults to participate in health-promotion workshops.** In early adulthood, people are likely to develop good or bad habits (diet, exercise, smoking, drinking, and drugs) that affect their health with significant consequences as they age.

Middle Adulthood: 40 to 64 Years

A host of physical changes present in the middle years come from the natural aging process. These changes can include skin wrinkles, yellowing teeth, loss and/or graying of hair, and weight gain. Alterations in the senses become evident in middle adulthood, especially changes in sight and hearing. Most people age 40 and older require reading glasses to help them see close objects and printed text.

By the 50s or 60s, the reduced blood supply to the eyes leads to a diminished visual field and increased blind spot. Sensitivity to high-pitched tones is usually the first decline noticed in hearing. The senses of taste and smell also decline in middle adulthood, leading many people to complain that food seems blander than it did years ago.

Another sign of aging is a reduction in height when spinal disks compress. Muscle strength is reduced in the middle years, although consistent exercise can increase muscle bulk. Coordination and reaction time are diminished with aging, although experience and knowledge can compensate for these changes.

Menopause for women usually begins between the ages of 45 and 55 and introduces several frustrating challenges. The decrease of estrogen production may result in nausea, fatigue, insomnia, hot flashes, vaginal dryness, and other symptoms. Women might consider the use of hormone replacement therapy (HRT) under the advice of a primary care provider.

Men experience a decrease in levels of testosterone over time, leaving them less fertile than in their younger years. While most men maintain their ability to father a child as they age, about 5 percent of men at age 40 experience erectile dysfunction (also known as impotence), which means they are unable to achieve or maintain an erection for a satisfying sexual experience. Many health conditions, use of alcohol or drugs, smoking, or anxiety may contribute to impotence. Consulting a healthcare provider is a good direction for men to pursue if there is a concern about physical changes.

Most men and women continue to be relatively healthy in their middle years. The most common serious health issues include diabetes, depression, anxiety, arthritis, heart disease, hypertension, and cancer. Cognitive abilities also remain relatively stable in the middle adult years. According to Erikson, the middle adult confronts the tasks of working out the conflict between generativity and stagnation.[10] Generativity refers to the guidance the middle adult can offer to the next generation through parenting, teaching, and mentoring. Stagnation occurs when the adult is inactive and focuses only on self-interests, leading to a life that can feel very small.

How can the congregation support middle-aged adults?

- **Host a series of discussions on specific health concerns.** This age group has a greater interest in conditions that become increasingly common such as hypertension, stroke, heart disease, cancer, osteoporosis, and diabetes. Here the focus should be on reducing risk or optimizing outcomes if the condition already exists.

- **Establish support groups for caregivers**. This phase of life is often called the "sandwich generation" because many middle-aged adults find themselves caring for both their children and their parents. Their ability to vent and learn from others in this difficult stage is particularly valuable.

- **Create opportunities for members to remain active.** Activities like walking groups, yoga classes, Pilates, and weight training provide a means to focus on physical and social health at little to no cost.

- **Start a 55+ monthly gathering for informative presentations and fellowship.** A drop-in-style format allows flexibility for attenders.

Late Adulthood: 65+ Years

People are living longer and are healthier today than ever before, and the number of people over the age of 65 continues to expand with the aging of the baby boomers. This is an especially critical age group in the context of the local church. Though the brain does lose mass over a lifetime, nerve cells and their connections actually increase through the 70s. Dendrites are the part of nerve cells in the brain that help carry messages. The exciting news is that older adults have the ability to maintain and expand intellectually.

There is a slowing in the ability to process as we age. Older adults may experience deteriorating senses of sight and hearing. Day and night vision, even with glasses, may be weakened. Cataracts, which are cloudy areas in the lenses of the eyes, can cause blurred vision, although surgical removal of cataracts has a high rate of success. Hearing aids are available to help older adults, and advancing technology has improved their effectiveness. A reduction in the ability to smell and taste is also common for older adults.

Strength, coordination, and reaction time are reduced with aging, though this can vary from person to person. Regular exercise is the best medicine for limiting decline with age. Weight training, stretching, walking, yoga, and tai chi are just a few of the many excellent options for older adults to maintain muscle strength and flexibility. Sexual activity can continue in later life, though usually with less frequency than in previous years. The most common causes of death in the elderly are heart disease, cancer, and respiratory disease. Chronic conditions are more common including arthritis, hypertension, hearing impairment, and heart conditions.

The key issue of this stage of life is "integrity versus despair."[11] At this stage, older adults begin to review their lives. A person who is satisfied with their life achieves integrity or wholeness. Alternately, a person who can find no meaning in their life will experience despair.

Adults who are healthy, financially secure, active, and connected to a social circle of family and friends usually have the best adjustment to retirement. For many, the role of grandparent or great-grandparent is a fulfilling component of their lives. Of course today, many older adults stay in the workforce, either for necessity to make ends meet or by choice because their work enriches their lives.

Older adults continue to live in the community, often with a spouse or other family members. Sixty percent of people 85 years and older actually live alone. It may be surprising that only 4 percent of people age 65 and older live in nursing homes. Most people prefer to live independently in late adulthood, but it is important to assess the quality and condition of each person's living situation individually.

How can the congregation support older adults?

- **See recommendations for middle-aged adults.**
- **Establish home visits for housebound seniors.** Mobility might become an issue, so social check-ins can lighten spirits and provide an early warning system if the senior needs medical attention.
- **Develop a transportation program to help those who are unable to drive get to their medical appointments.**
- **Offer targeted discussions related to change.** Older adults need to cope with multiple losses, including physical changes, retirement, and deaths of loved ones. Providing a safe space can offer comfort and instill hope.

What is the significance of human development to your faith organization? Every faith community is in a different place in terms of what is most appropriate to its members. Are you a congregation teeming with infants, children, or teens? Or are your members more seasoned? Perhaps you are a large church with health-related needs that cross all ages and life stages. As you determine where to begin with your health ministry, remember that you can build from the area that targets the greatest need to a broader array of services and groups in years to come.

 Are You Health Aware?

- What are the ages of your members?

- Are there developing trends, such as a growing senior population or more infants and children?

- Within your larger community, where can your church provide support, such as a space where older adults can gather or forums to discuss pressing issues like drug abuse or teen suicide?

- Are there members of your church who have expertise in one or more of the age groups? How can you best leverage their gifts and talents?

Health-Aware Checklist

____ Do you know the age distribution of your church membership?

____ Have you identified activities, groups, or services that exist at each developmental level in your church and how your congregation participates in them?

____ How can you use these activities, groups, or services to reach out into the community?

____ Who in your congregation has expertise at different developmental stages?

____ Is there interest in starting a new group or support service?

 **Next Steps**

Right now we can:

Within three months, we will:

Our end-of-year goal is:

Table 2.1   Age Characteristics, Milestones, and Health Considerations

Age	Highlights	Health and Wellness Considerations	Actions for the Local Church
Prenatal to birth	• Is the baby desired or not? • Infertility issues • Miscarriage	• Mother's health key to baby's health • Postpartum depression • Birth defects • Low birth-weight baby	• Spiritual support • Encourage access of community resources for pregnant women
Birth to 3 years	• Period of rapid growth • Primitive responses dominate • Trust vs. mistrust (0–18 months) • Autonomy vs. shame/doubt (1–3 years)	• Consider developmental milestones and actions if delays noted. Early intervention is critical for best outcomes. • Assess for evidence of bonding between infant and parents.	• Offer parenting classes and support groups • Sponsor community experts for targeted workshops that relate to parents and children in this age group • Host online group where parents can ask questions and receive support

Age	Highlights	Health and Wellness Considerations	Actions for the Local Church
3 to 6 years	• Growth continues, though more slowly • Fine motor skills advance • Large motor skills include run, hop, skip, throw • Use symbols, classify objects • "Why" questions abound • Increased vocabulary, grammar, syntax • Initiative vs. guilt	• Risk for accidents increases • Sleep disturbances common • Bed-wetting may present • Active and imaginative playtime is critical • Assess for continued motor, language, emotional, and social development	• Offer parenting classes and support groups on topics of child safety, accident prevention, bed-wetting, discipline, sleep issues • Sponsor community experts for targeted workshops that relate to parents and children in this age group • Host online group where parents can ask questions and receive support
6 to 12 years	• Physical growth slows as motor skills and mental abilities expand • Problem-solving skills evolve • Developing moral code • Industry vs. inferiority	• Learning disabilities and attention deficit disorder identified in school-aged children • Watch for signs of abuse or depression • Nutrition, sleep, and exercise important	• Establish child-friendly, family-friendly sports programs • Sponsor nutrition and cooking workshops • Host parental support groups

Age	Highlights	Health and Wellness Considerations	Actions for the Local Church
13 to 18 years	• Significant physical, cognitive, emotional, and social changes • Puberty occurs (if not earlier) • Develop hypothetical-deductive reasoning • Moral development progresses to understanding of principles of fairness and justice • Search for self-identity	• Sexual orientation may be explored • High-risk behaviors may be present	• Sponsor concurrent but separate classes for teens and their parents on relevant topics • Keep a current list of qualified health providers, especially mental health
19 to 39 years	• Relatively healthy period • Intimacy vs. isolation	• Personal health choices (positive or negative) begin to be evident on level of health	• Host program to explore relationships • Sponsor health-promotion workshops
40 to 64 years	• Physical evidence of aging more apparent • Senses begin to be affected • Menopause for women and decreased testosterone in men • Generativity vs. stagnation	• Relatively healthy time, though increase in diabetes, depression, arthritis, heart disease, hypertension, and cancer	• Present sessions on specific health concerns • Establish support groups for caregivers • Host activity groups like yoga, walking, and/or weight training

Age	Highlights	Health and Wellness Considerations	Actions for the Local Church
65+	• Learning continues • Ability to process slows • Senses continue to decline • Integrity vs. despair • Retirement or change in hours worked	• Chronic conditions may impact lifestyle • Social interaction with friends and family important	• See 40–64 age group • Establish visits for homebound seniors • Develop transportation support • Offer discussion groups related to life changes

3

CARING PROFESSIONALS

"So that there should be no division in the body, but that its parts should have equal concern for each other."
—*1 Corinthians 12:25*

Edna was 77 years old and married to George, age 80. When George was diagnosed with early dementia and colon cancer at the same time, Edna was overwhelmed with all the doctor appointments and tests. Their children lived in different towns, and Edna wasn't sure she could handle it alone. The healthcare system seemed like an angry dog barking at her, and she didn't understand what to do to help George. Edna felt powerless.

Today's complex healthcare system can be scary for anyone but especially for the elderly and those with limited resources. Fear keeps people from practicing preventive health, such as going for regular checkups, getting a flu shot, or having the recommended screenings. Older people who need to downsize their homes or move closer to adult children for help often wait until a health crisis occurs, making alternate living decisions more difficult on them and their families.

Understanding key components in healthcare, how the system is designed to work, settings for care, and who the health team members are can help allay fears and make people feel they have some control over tough situations related to illness.

Navigating the Healthcare System

The healthcare system is complicated, even for doctors and nurses. A local church ministry team armed with even basic information can help families view themselves as the center of their own healthcare teams. They are co-managers of their illnesses or injuries and have a right to the facts surrounding their care. Encourage families to understand the plan of care for themselves or a loved one. Help them ask good questions and encourage them to keep a record of communications so they don't forget details. Suggest that they ask for things in writing if that helps. Counsel them to get treatment at facilities they trust and from doctors who listen to them and with whom they feel comfortable. Remind them that it is okay to go elsewhere for care if they don't feel the treatment is sufficient. Help them understand the importance of doing their part by following a doctor or primary care provider's treatment plan. If a plan is not working, encourage them to let their provider know. There are several ways a ministry team could handle this within the local church:

- Plan healthcare workshops using medical people from within or outside the church.
- Provide printed material about advocating for yourself in the healthcare system.
- Offer one-on-one help, if needed.
- Make regular calls to support people with healthcare issues.
- Print cards containing helpful tips to keep pertinent reminders available for quick access.
- Encourage individuals to write down the questions they want to ask the doctor or nurse.

- Have the faith community nurse or a volunteer health provider in the congregation accompany a person to their doctor's visits, if needed.
- Ask the hospital to assign a patient advocate, if needed.

Care Settings

A crisis or accident is what often first sends a person to the hospital to seek care. This results in what is called **acute care**, which is what most hospitals specialize in. When a person needs a longer period of recovery or rehabilitation, they may be sent to **rehabilitation care**, which is its own unit in the hospital or located in a separate long-term-care facility. Rehabilitation care is for patients who can tolerate three hours of therapy or more per day and who generally have a goal of returning home. If a little help at home is needed, **home care** may be an option. Home care is managed through an agency that specializes in caring for people at home. A person may get nursing help, therapy, homemaker services, and medical equipment through a home-care agency. Most of these settings are covered by private insurance and Medicare.

For aging adults who need assistance, **assisted living** can provide 24-hour access to a nurse while still allowing individuals to live mostly independently, with some assistance in activities of daily living. Assisted-living facilities typically provide meals, laundry services, transportation, and social activities. If longer-term skilled nursing services and care are needed, then **long-term care** (nursing home placement) may be an option. Many nursing homes offer specialized units for those with dementia, called **memory care** units.

The local church can help by providing the church's contact information when someone is admitted to a care center. With the person's permission, an update can also be added to the church bulletin and/or a regular newsletter. Send encouragement cards. Make a personal visit. Even the smallest remembrance can make a big difference to a person in crisis.

When George, from the opening illustration, had surgery to remove the cancer in his colon, Edna saw many, many people come in and out of the room in the intensive care unit (ICU). She later told her daughter, "I have no idea who all these people are! There are so many going in and out all day. I just can't keep track of them." If Edna had known the roles of typical team members in the hospital, it might have made it easier for her to cope with George's recovery and participate better in his rehabilitation plan.

- How would you help someone reduce the stress and anxiety connected to the issues identified here?

George went to inpatient rehabilitation after two weeks in the hospital. At this time, he was assigned a nurse who acted as a case manager and helped Edna and George understand the plan for his recovery. The nurse was able to answer Edna's questions and act as a go-between for Edna and the rest of the healthcare team members. Edna felt less anxious as she saw George improving in therapy. She felt more comfortable asking her questions because she was welcomed as part of George's recovery team.

- How would you help someone know who the important go-to people were?
- How would you help Edna and George use this person to reduce their anxiety?
- What role could ministry volunteers fulfill in supporting family members in these types of situations?

Trying to get the right help and answers to healthcare needs can be a challenge for anyone. Encourage your faith community to take charge of their own health by practicing prevention such as immunizations and screenings. If someone does have to be hospitalized, encourage them to know their rights and responsibilities as a patient and to strive to be the co-manager of their own health along with their healthcare team.

Table 3.1 summarizes the key team members you might expect to see in a hospital and/or rehabilitation setting. When patients are cared for by a team of experts, they recover faster and better. Each health professional brings a unique set of skills to the care of the patient, and they all work together toward common goals to help the patient get back to the maximum state of wellness possible after an illness or injury. This group of health experts is called the inter-professional team, or interdisciplinary team. Although there are many more professionals who may help in case of catastrophic injury or illness, these are foundational team members.

Table 3.1   **The Basic Healthcare Team***

Who They Are	What They Do
Physician (doctor)	Coordinates the medical care of the patient; diagnoses illness and prescribes treatment, including medications; a patient may have multiple physicians who each specialize in a different area
Nurse	Provides direct care, including administering medications and other forms of treatment; teaches the patient and family; helps with discharge planning; is an advocate for the patient and family to the rest of the team
Physical therapist	Works with walking and returning muscles to their best function; is an expert on muscles, bones, movement
Occupational therapist	Works more with the upper body; helps with activities of daily living such as showering, toileting, dressing, cooking, and returning to work
Speech therapist	Helps patients who have speech and swallowing problems; also works to help those with cognitive issues, such as memory problems
Psychologist	Provides counseling and behavioral management interventions for patient and family
Social worker	Helps with the social situation, such as living arrangements, ordering equipment needed at home, dealing with insurance, and discharge planning
Dietitian	Gives recommendations for appropriate diet
Spiritual advisor	Typically a clergy member, gives spiritual support and/or guidance to the patient and family

*There are many other health professionals who may be added to a patient's team, depending on the diagnosis and need.

Are You Health Aware?

- How many individuals in your faith community live in a long-term-care facility or assisted living?

- Who maintains contact with or visits individuals who are in the hospital or nursing homes?

- What processes are in place to minister to the sick and disabled in your community?

Health-Aware Checklist

_____ Do you have a weekly prayer list for those who are experiencing health problems?

_____ Do you have a ministry to the sick or ill or homebound?

_____ What nursing homes in the area have your congregational members residing in them? What types of ministries does your faith community engage in these settings? Is there more you could be doing?

 Next Steps

Right now we can:

Within three months, we will:

Our end-of-year goal is:

4

DIVERSITY AND HEALTH

"If it is possible, as far as it depends on you, live at peace with everyone."
—Romans 12:18

I recall hearing Marilyn Laszlo, a Bible translator who spent more than twenty-five years among a tribe in Papua New Guinea, tell the story of the first funeral she viewed as a young missionary in that country. She recounted her horror in watching the tribesmen bury a young boy who was unconscious but still breathing. Marilyn told the witch doctor conducting the death ritual that the boy was not dead yet; therefore, they should not bury him alive. But the witch doctor told her harshly, "Be quiet, white woman. You do not know anything!" This was Marilyn's introduction to the view of death in the Sepik Iwam culture. At that time, they defined death as being unable to move or speak on one's own, not by the signs that Marilyn had been taught, such as the prolonged absence of breathing and heartbeat.

Just like Marilyn, we may be strangers in a culture that is foreign to us. Most of us will not have to feel the extreme conflict that Marilyn did in dealing with such a heart-rending situation. But we will need to observe, listen, and learn. In order to minister effectively to other people, we need to understand ourselves first, and then learn about others, and how we are similar to and different from them.

The health practices of a person's culture of origin or the culture in which the person lives often influence current health practices. In order to promote health within your communities and congregations, you need to understand what is meant by "culture" and how it affects the way we live. Several components of cultural diversity and health will be discussed in this chapter. You will also learn strategies and ministry ideas to help you become more culturally sensitive, both as an individual and within your faith community.

Culture

There are many different ways to define culture. Generally, the word refers to common attitudes, beliefs, feelings, and values shared by a group of people. These influence behavior and social norms. Several components of culture include race, religion, gender, age, sexual orientation, living arrangements, finances, education, employment, and uniqueness. When you are trying to understand a culture that is different from yours, it helps to consider each of these factors. This chapter outlines those strong forces that make up a culture, and gives you some clear suggestions about how this new knowledge can help your congregation achieve better health, happier lives, and a unique place of ministry in your community.

Race and Ethnicity

Many people think of culture as a person's racial background. Race is certainly part of culture, but it is only one aspect. The word *race* refers to a group of people whose identity is based on physical appearance. *Ethnicity* encompasses race, language, dress, history, and the sense of being part of a unique group. There are several major ethnic or cultural groups within the United States, including

Anglo or European-American, African American, Hispanic, Asian, and Native American.

- What ethnic groups are most common in your congregation's geographic location? Does your church membership reflect ethnic diversity? Why or why not?

Gender

Many health problems are associated more with one gender than another. For example, osteoporosis is more common in female patients, while spinal cord injuries are more common among male patients. Women are more likely to be providers of healthcare than men, and women have a longer life span than men. The statistical list goes on and on.

Considering gender issues can help you plan a more relevant and useful congregational health program. If your group is largely female, think about the group's unique healthcare needs or where they would most likely wish to do outreach ministries. Perhaps you would include more educational programs on subjects that uniquely affect women, such as menopause, breast cancer, incontinence, pregnancy, or child safety. On the other hand, if your target group is predominantly male, consider programs such as stress reduction, prevention of heart disease, preventing sports injuries, or prostate cancer screening.

Age

Your congregation may range in age from newborns to the frail elderly. Other churches may have a larger percentage of older adults. The particular situation of each congregation will definitely influence the types of ministries in which the church may want to invest. Older adults experience more chronic illnesses, disabilities, and usually more hospitalizations and health complications. A growing trend in the U.S. is grandparents raising their young grandchildren who live with them. This responsibility presents an entirely unique ministry opportunity within the church, since grandparents engaged in this service need much support from their friends or those in their community.

Children are prone to accidents. A child-rearing family has different needs than an older couple whose children are grown and have moved away. Adolescents face their own particular hazards, including peer pressure, bullying, social media pressures, the need for acceptance, and the temptations of drugs, sex, and alcohol use.

- Which age groups have the greatest needs in your church?
- Consider bringing in a speaker from a local medical or nursing school to talk about the aging process and how to combat the effects of old age.
- How can your church have an impact in the schools in your area?

Ministry Idea

Consider this wonderful ministry suggestion by a dear friend who is a grandmother. She has partnered with her local Child Protective Services (CPS) agency to provide a backpack to each child at the time they are removed from their parents' home into the foster care system. In each backpack (which is colorful and in a popular theme for boys or girls), she puts:

- A soft blanket that she sews herself in a popular theme for kids.
- A stuffed animal.
- A toothbrush, toothpaste, shampoo, deodorant, and other hygiene items.
- Small, nonperishable snack items.
- A bottle of water.

She makes the backpacks in advance and takes them ten at a time to the local CPS agency, who are immensely appreciative to be able to provide displaced children with this gift of something that can be their own when, often, they are removed from their homes without being allowed to take anything. Imagine the comfort this gift gives to kids in such a frightening time.

Sexual Orientation

Sexual orientation is a sensitive subject for many church congregations, but it is one that cannot be ignored in today's society. Church members can be sensitive to differences in sexual orientation without condoning certain practices. Too often, differences in sexual orientation or gender identity are the source of estrangement and stigma within families and churches. Because it is not a subject that is often discussed graciously in the church community, families in the midst of this struggle often feel isolated and ostracized.

Single mother Ann has just been told by her twenty-year-old son, Jason, that he is gay and plans to marry another man. Ann raised her son in the church, but now she feels that she failed to convey the truths that are most important to her. She blames herself for her son's lack of a father figure, but she cannot accept the lifestyle he has chosen. Ann's pain runs deep. She cannot turn to the people she would ordinarily turn to for help. She is unable to share her thoughts and her grief with the people in her church because she is embarrassed and ashamed. She also fears that Jason will contract HIV because of his sexual behaviors. So she decides to cut off all contact with him until he changes.

- *What feelings would both Ann and Jason have in this situation?*
- *How could your congregation reach out to Ann or Jason?*

Pastors who are comfortable talking about sexual orientation can introduce the subject in a sensitive way to others. Talk with your pastor about questions or problems. In the case study above, Ann should have felt that she could speak with her pastor about her feelings. Always listen first to the person who is hurting. Use non-judgmental language. If this is a prevalent issue in your congregation, consider scheduling informational presentations about these issues that could be helpful.

Religion and Spirituality

A distinction between the terms *religion* and *spirituality* may be helpful here. Religion refers to organized worship or faith, like what takes place in the denomination or faith tradition you belong to, such as Catholic, Baptist, Methodist, Buddhist, Muslim, or Jewish. Spirituality is more general, referring to one's own feeling of being connected to a higher power. Thus, a person could call oneself spiritual without being religious or affiliating with any one church, temple, or denomination.

Religion and spirituality are key components of most cultures. Religious practices and traditions provide continuity, help define our lives, and provide help and comfort in times of crisis. Spiritual beliefs are closely linked to particular practices. For example, in many Christian denominations, baptism represents the cleansing of sin and marks the person's entry into the faith community. Catholics believe it is essential that a priest anoint a sick person prior to death. Most Buddhists are cremated. Hindus and Buddhists believe in reincarnation. The use of alcohol is forbidden in Islam and Mormonism. Jehovah's Witnesses are excommunicated if they receive a blood transfusion. Orthodox Jews eat only kosher foods.

We must keep the important influence of religion and spirituality in mind to be effective in service to others, even when we do not agree with or share the beliefs and practices.

Finances, Education, and Employment

Finances, education, and employment have closely related influences on culture and may also help determine a person's health status. For example, as a person becomes better educated, they may be able to get a better-paying job and more insurance benefits, thus positively influencing their health and that of the family. Conversely, if a man lacks education and takes a job working in a factory from which he is then laid off, or a woman lacks education and ends up working in a fast-food restaurant with low wages and few benefits, their finances will suffer.

Those in lower socioeconomic groups often have poorer access to medical facilities and healthcare than other groups. The uninsured and underinsured often suffer from illnesses and diseases that are left untreated because they lack the funds to pay for needed health services. Insurance is costly, and there are probably people in your community and even your congregation without health insurance. They do not have to be older or even out of work. Some teenagers make just enough to support themselves but do not receive health benefits from their employer. A struggling single parent who puts herself through school and works part time may not have health benefits for her children. A man who has lost his job may no longer be able to afford the out-of-pocket expenses for medical coverage for his pregnant wife. Each of these situations can thrust a family into a lifetime of trying to pay back medical expenses from a catastrophic illness or accident.

Education and socioeconomic status are closely related. One often influences the other. Better-educated people are usually in a higher socioeconomic group. But education need not be the privilege of the few. Your church can be a place of education about health practices and disease prevention. You can teach people how to reduce risk factors, how to get help when they need it, and how to take medicine regularly. As an added benefit, your congregation may find that, as gifts and grants come in to assist these efforts, it becomes financially stronger.

Employment is another factor in the cultural equation that becomes especially important in times of economic trouble. People often derive a sense of satisfaction and even a sense of identity from their jobs. If that job is lost, personal uncertainty can lead to depression and poor health. Fortunately, funding for clinics in underserved areas has increased at both state and national levels. Often termed clinics for the "working poor," these sites provide basic healthcare services for people who cannot afford more traditional health plans. Your congregation can help people whose finances keep them from getting the healthcare they need.

Questions to Ask to Help Those without Medical Coverage

- What are your community resources? Is there a free clinic in your area?
- What services do they provide and for whom?
- Does the person qualify for Medicaid (a state-run health program for the poor and disabled)?
- Who in your community could help this person find a job?
- What skills does the person have that could be useful?
- Is there a job in your church for that person?

Ministry Ideas

- Develop links and connections with agencies in your community that provide necessary help. Keep in mind that there may be programs already in place but not well advertised.
- Invite a speaker from a helping facility to be a guest at your next women's luncheon or other demographic-specific gathering.

Living Arrangements

The place we call home helps define who we are. In the United States, the way our home is arranged helps tell others what we value and who we are. Our homes often reflect our personal tastes and desires, the things we treasure. People within one community often have similar housing and even similar living arrangements. We all know when we're in a rich neighborhood or a poor one. And even where people may live in straw huts, those huts are the living style of that community.

The most striking example of how living arrangements influence culture is that of the homeless. Homelessness is a widespread problem in most major cities. You may even be able to think of someone you have seen in your own town who walks about the streets during the day pushing a shopping cart or carrying multiple bags or rummaging through the trash. The homeless are typically stigmatized by society, and they often have limited access to healthcare. For many, healthcare may seem like a luxury since they also lack consistent and reliable access to food, shelter, clothing, and transportation. They may live in cardboard boxes, in alleys, by the river, or under bridges. They might sleep in homeless shelters or on a bench in the train station or at the airport. In certain cities, the homeless population is so large that city workers pass out cardboard boxes each evening for people to sleep in. Other cities confine their homeless to specific neighborhoods to hide them from more wealthy areas.

Many people who become homeless have physical, emotional, and/or psychological problems. Others were working professionals who fell on bad times and were unable to recover because they lacked sufficient resources or help. Homelessness is a growing area for church ministry.

Ministry Ideas

- Find out if there are homeless people living in your community and how widespread the problem is.
- Talk to local social service agencies about what is being done to address the problem of homelessness.
- Become familiar with your community resources including food pantries, job-finding assistance, free meals, transportation, bus tokens, pregnancy assistance centers, homeless shelters, and substance abuse treatment agencies. Work with your local agencies and government to offer help.
- Make regular donations to food pantries, or set one up in your church. If your church has a food pantry already, find out how you can volunteer there.
- Join forces with other congregations to provide shelter to the homeless in your gym or fellowship area. Each church

can take one night of the week and have some volunteers to help supervise while others make meals or pack lunches for the homeless.

- Ask local agencies to donate bus passes, restaurants to give free meal coupons, and vendors to offer free services such as haircuts.

Personal Uniqueness

People are unique, and some have obvious differences that may cause them to be left out in a group setting. It may be a physical deformity such as a birth defect, or a disability such as cerebral palsy, visual impairment, or the use of adaptive equipment such as a cane or walker or wheelchair. Anything that makes a person feel different from the cultural norm can cause them to separate from the group. Additionally, some professionals believe that those with common illnesses or diseases form their own type of cultural group based on the processes they must go through in the course of their lives.

Recognizing Your Own Cultural Heritage

The first step to becoming more sensitive to the cultures of others is to be familiar with your own. This task should be purposefully undertaken in order to develop cultural sensitivity to others. Consider some of the following questions about your own cultural heritage:

- What are some of your family traditions? How long have you practiced them? How much do you value your traditions?
- Where did your grandparents grow up? What is their country of origin? What generation are you? (For example, first-generation Americans were born in the United States after their parents migrated from another country.)

- What religious practices are important to you? What religious dates do you observe? What special holidays or celebrations are unique to your family?
- How important is extended family to you?
- What is your standard of living?
- What is your general health status? How much do you value the healthcare system?
- Do you have unique health practices (e.g., dietary restrictions or the use of certain folk medicines)?

Appreciating and sharing cultural differences offers a tremendous richness. Exploring other cultures and other faiths helps us clarify and appreciate our own in addition to providing a wealth of knowledge about others.

Most people believe their own culture is the best, but that attitude may spring from prejudices such as racism, ageism, and sexism. By knowing yourself and the significance of your own culture, you may be better prepared to recognize and respect those who come from different cultures.

American Cultures and Health

It was important at the beginning of this chapter to present information about other cultures in order to understand how culture influences health practices. A basic understanding of the five major ethnic groups in the United States may also be helpful. In order to describe them, we must generalize, but the reader is encouraged to accept that each culture has a set of subcultures and that each subculture can be unique. Do not stereotype anyone whom you encounter, but use this basic information as a springboard for inquiring into the cultures of people in your sphere of influence. Each person is unique and should not be forced into a predetermined mold based on race or ethnicity. The intent of this section is simply to provide some basic factors about each of the five major groups—Anglo-Americans, Black Americans, Hispanics, Asian Americans, and Native Americans—and to suggest some examples of how culture influences their health practices. There are health disparities within these groups that impact wellness and accessibility to care.

Table 4.1   American Ethnic Groups and Health Considerations

Ethnic group	Origin	Subcultures	General characteristics	Health disparities
Anglo or European Americans	Caucasian white, non-Hispanic	Jewish, Italian, French, Irish, German, Polish	Higher educational levels, better incomes, better health, longer life span; strong ties to country of origin; value beauty, wealth, success, health, independence; family-oriented; value traditional Western medicine and science; common religion is Christianity (both Catholic and Protestant)	Provides standard for other ethnic groups related to health disparities

Ethnic group	Origin	Subcultures	General characteristics	Health disparities
Black Americans	African continent, roots in slavery, Caribbean	American-born; Jamaican, Haitian, Nigerian, Dominican	Historically suffered discrimination and cruelty; higher poverty rate; strong social support through family; religious upbringing and church affiliation are often strong; common religion is Protestant Christianity; respect their elderly; use home remedies for illness; may mistrust the healthcare system due to negative experiences and a pattern of mistreatment by the healthcare system	More chronic illness; higher rate of high blood pressure, heart disease, stroke (and at a younger age); often have less access to healthcare resources; more likely to use the emergency room than a primary care physician
Hispanics	Latin descent or Spanish-speaking origin	Mexican, Cuban, Puerto Rican, Southern or Central American	Emphasize interdependence of family; self-care less important than family providing care; may use homeopathic remedies; may view illness as punishment for sins; common religion is Catholicism	Diabetes; heart disease; higher blood pressure; tuberculosis; cervical cancer; may have more barriers to accessing healthcare services

Ethnic group	Origin	Subcultures	General characteristics	Health disparities
Asian Americans	China, India, Philippines, Vietnam, Korea, Middle East, native Hawaiian and Pacific Islanders, Japan, Pakistan	Asian Indian, Chinese, Filipino, Japanese, Korean, Pakistani, Vietnamese	Place high value on personal connections; incorporate or practice Traditional Chinese Medicine (TCM); beliefs influenced by Buddhism, Confucianism, and Taoism; many claim no religion; all things in the body are from balance of yin-yang (opposing forces); treatments focus on restoring balance between these hot/cold forces	Liver cancer; stomach cancer; tuberculosis; hepatitis; end-stage renal disease; certain subgroups (native Hawaiian and Pacific Islanders) have more obesity
Native Americans	First settlers in America; did not migrate	About 500 different tribes, each with own customs; Cherokee and Navajo are most common	Have a naturalistic approach to health and illness; health is a balance of mind, body, spirit; legends of sacred spirits; health related to earth, wind, fire; honor and care for elders	Diabetes; alcoholism; tuberculosis; suicide; younger life expectancy

Increasing Cultural Sensitivity in the Congregation

People can feel frustrated and helpless when dealing with other cultures. We may have trouble accepting other cultural practices because of how they conflict with our own beliefs and value system. The best way to remedy our blindness to our prejudice against other cultures is to observe and listen to people who are different from us and to examine personal feelings about our own cultural roots. Then we can begin to appreciate others. Members of the congregation should try to learn all that they can about differing cultural and religious beliefs so that when issues arise, they will take advantage of a great opportunity to educate one another. Make sure this sensitizing process is undertaken in a non-threatening, non-judgmental manner. Here are some suggestions for getting started:

- Keep the main goal of your health program at the forefront of the discussion, and do not allow individual agendas to detract from that goal.
- Develop your own cultural sensitivity, and encourage church members to be open and hospitable to people who are different from them.
- Devise ways to resolve conflict.
- Make a plan to include various cultural traditions in your church activities or programs.
- Invite your international missionaries to teach about the cultures in which they live and serve.

 ## Are You Health Aware?

Evaluate your own cultural sensitivity:

- Do I accept others who are different from me?

- If a person who is different from me comes to visit my church, do I go up and introduce myself?

- How do I feel when I see a homeless person? Or someone begging in front of a store?

- Do I harbor any negative feelings, thoughts, or attitudes toward people of another race, the elderly, teens, children, or the opposite gender?

- Would I be willing to serve in a soup kitchen during the holidays?

- Is there anything I am doing now to help those less fortunate than me? What else could I be doing?

- How do my children react to people who have a physical deformity? To the poor? To those who live in a run-down house?

- Do I believe that being sensitive to people who are different from me is part of the mission of my church? Part of my personal mission? Something I should be doing to demonstrate my faith?

 ## Health-Aware Checklist

____ What groups in your community are most in need of spiritual care and resources?

_____ Are there overnight shelters available for the homeless population in your area? Places to get warm or stay cool? Places that serve food? Places to shower? Clinics that offer free healthcare?

_____ Is there a prison nearby? Does your church have an outreach ministry there?

_____ How could you help the local pregnancy assistance center?

_____ What is your church doing to minister to single pregnant mothers?

_____ How could you help those who consider abortion because they have no hope or resources?

✓ Next Steps

Right now we can:

Within three months, we will:

Our end-of-year goal is:

PART TWO

Developing a Health-Aware Ministry and Community

5

BEFORE YOU BEGIN

*"There is a time for everything, and a season
for every activity under the heavens."*
—*Ecclesiastes 3:1*

Motivation and Goals

Because a health ministry requires wholehearted commitment, ownership, and participation, the church must be as clear as possible about its level of motivation from the start. Worldwide, communities of faith consider the health of the individual and the collective congregation as a component of their higher mission. For Christians, the centrality of health and healing is evident in biblical teachings and in current congregational practices. Tending the mind, body, and spirit of parishioners is embedded in the church's rich history of compassionate caring.

Still, it is important to understand why *your* congregation chooses to devote time, space, and money to a health ministry when these resources are always at a premium. Most congregations must be deliberate in the way they use their resources. So before you begin, consider these questions:

- Is the idea for the health ministry program coming from many members of your congregation or only a few?
- Is there a broad demand for programming from all age groups or only from one group?

- Are these requests for health education programs, health screenings, and health promotion, or do people want actual diagnosis and treatment options?
- Are there members of the congregation who are qualified to organize and oversee such programs?
- Who are the members who are interested in serving in the health ministry program?
- How supportive of a health ministry are the members of the congregation's professional staff?
- Do lay leaders of the church support this idea?

Answering these questions and others that might be specific to your congregation is essential to clarifying the vision of your church's health ministry. To gain this information you might consider distributing an electronic survey to your members. You could meet with groups that already exist in your church to hear their opinions. Your pastoral team and lay leaders may have significant insight into the most pressing health issues among the members with whom they have contact on a routine basis.

Assuming you find that you are ready, you must clarify the health-related goals of the congregation. For example, if many members of your congregation are uninsured or underinsured and do not have their own healthcare providers, your goals probably would include the active treatment of illness or assisting in securing insurance. If most of your members do have adequate insurance already, your ministry may want to concentrate on improving overall health and promoting positive lifestyle changes.

Whatever the specific needs of individual programs, most health ministries will share the following goals:

- Improving overall health through health education and health-promotion activities.
- Preventing potential disease through risk appraisals, screening programs, and disease-prevention activities.
- Promoting wellness and well-being.

- Diagnosing and treating new cases of illness.
- Maintaining an optimal level of health with known illnesses or conditions.

A health ministry program may have a single emphasis, or it may be multipurpose. There is no one way to have a successful program, but all successful programs begin with a clear vision and established goals.

Details, Details, Details

With an identified vision and set goals, you move into the practical issues of creating a health ministry program. What organizational structure will your program use? To answer that, you may need a little history.

The movement toward pairing the traditional healthcare community with the faith community began in the late 1960s with the work of Rev. Granger Westberg. These early efforts have crystallized today into parish or faith community nursing. The Westberg Institute for Faith Community Nursing (westberginstitute.org) can be a helpful resource to beginning your health ministry.

As you consider the organizational structure of your program, you will need to address additional questions. While your list may be longer, here are some of those questions:

- Who will be responsible for your health program? What qualifications do you require?
- To whom will your health coordinator report?
- Will the health coordinator be paid or unpaid? If paid, how will you raise the funds?
- Will you collaborate with other churches? Or agencies?
- What resources will you need, including space, equipment, personnel, and materials?
- How will you train volunteers?
- Have you considered liability insurance?

- Where will you refer persons who need more care than you can provide?
- What documentation system will you use?
- How will physicians and other healthcare providers be involved?

How you answer these questions will be critical to the success of your program. Remember that it is better to start small rather than trying to address all goals or issues at once. For example, it might be best to start with one significant issue like diabetes or better eating habits instead of setting up programs for heart health, memory care, addictions, and the like. There will be lessons to learn through the early stages that can be applied as your program continues to grow. Also, as you evidence the value of focusing on wellness or health concerns, the support and engagement in these programs will continue to grow. Remember that this is a project of faith and grit!

In this chapter, we have asked more questions than we have answered, which is appropriate since no one but you can set up your health ministry program. The point we want to make is that your congregation must be fully engaged in the program. In order to be fully engaged, members need to feel responsible for their health. Such responsibility will take some learning and change, since it departs from the way healthcare is generally practiced today in the United States. A health ministry model places at the center the person who attends to his or her physical, emotional, social, and spiritual well-being. The health ministry program empowers members of the church to take charge of their own health!

Are You Health Aware?

After answering the questions presented earlier in this chapter, you will have a clearer idea about your church's health-aware status.

Health-Aware Checklist

_____ Who might be responsible for your health program? What qualifications would you require?

_____ To whom would your health coordinator report?

_____ Would you use a paid or unpaid health coordinator? If paid, how would you raise the funds?

_____ Would you collaborate with other churches or agencies?

_____ What resources would you need, including space, equipment, personnel, and materials?

_____ How could you train volunteers?

_____ Have you considered liability insurance?

_____ Where would you refer persons who need more care than you can provide?

_____ What documentation system might you use?

_____ How will physicians and other healthcare providers be involved?

 ## Next Steps

Right now we can:

Within three months, we will:

Our end-of-year goal is:

6

BUILDING YOUR HEALTH MINISTRY TEAM

"Therefore, my dear brothers and sisters, stand firm. Let nothing move you. Always give yourselves fully to the work of the Lord, because you know that your labor in the Lord is not in vain."
—1 Corinthians 15:58

Sarah was an experienced nurse who taught at the local university. During church one Sunday an usher called her to the back entryway, where she saw an older man named Bill on the floor. He was pale, sweating, short of breath, and clutching his chest. Sarah recognized the signs as a possible heart attack and directed the usher to call 911. As Sarah assessed Bill, knowing it could be a life-threatening situation, she tried to help him stay calm.

He said to Sarah, "I can't hold on." Then he raised his left arm in the air, opened his hand as if taking the hand of someone Sarah could not see, and said, "I have to go." At that moment, Bill stopped breathing. The paramedics arrived and began CPR. They continued during the ambulance ride to the hospital, but they could not save Bill's life. Bill entered heaven that very day. Sarah believed that, when he reached out just before he stopped breathing, Bill was taking the hand of Jesus.

After this event, Sarah felt called to put together a health ministry team at her church. Although she had long felt the need, Bill's heart attack and death illustrated the urgent importance of emphasizing health promotion as well as putting a better plan in place for emergencies that may occur in church. Sarah wasn't sure where to start, so she conferred with other nurses in her church.

Building your health ministry team can feel like an overwhelming task. However, the scripture at the beginning of this chapter assures us that our "labor for the Lord is not in vain." This chapter will give you some practical tips for putting together your team and moving toward achieving your goals for your congregation.

Identify a Small Group of Interested People

Isn't it fascinating that Jesus chose only twelve men to help him begin his ministry on earth? This small group of untrained men who were mentored by the Master changed the world forever. As you start to build your team, consider how many people you want to help with strategic planning and to form your team. Too large a group is hard to get together, but too small a group makes for a heavier workload. What is the ideal number for your team? This may depend on the size of your congregation or the number of health professionals who want to be part of the team.

Next, consider *whom* you want to be part of this team. Not all those involved need to be health professionals, but all members should have a passion for health promotion and health ministry. You should have a variety of ages and experience levels as well as a balance between men and women if possible. Some key members to include on the team might be:

- Physicians
- Nurses or nursing assistants
- EMTs, paramedics, or other emergency/first-responder personnel
- Therapists
- Security personnel
- Pastor or counselor

- Social workers
- Psychologists or psychiatrists
- Dietitians
- Anyone else who expresses an interest and wishes to serve

Set Up Your First Meeting

So you have identified a small group of people who might be interested in being part of your team. Now it is time to plan your first meeting. Here are some practical suggestions for this first meeting:

Set a time when most of the interested people can attend.

This may mean a Sunday after church services, a Friday night after work, or a Saturday breakfast time. Aim for the time that allows the most people who expressed interest to be present. The first meeting is often a brainstorming session where many great ideas are shared, so you'll want to recruit as much brainpower as possible.

Keep it short.

Develop an agenda and stick to it. The first meeting should be no more than 60–90 minutes. The major purpose is to ascertain the level of interest of volunteers, establish a clear purpose for the group, set some initial goals, and agree upon a regular meeting time. Here is an example of an agenda you might use for the first meeting.

Prayer and devotions:	10 minutes
Introduce participants:	5 minutes
Explain the purpose of the program:	10 minutes
Discussion and brainstorming:	30 minutes
Set goals for the year:	10 minutes
Set meeting dates and times:	5 minutes

Have a plan.

At this meeting, explain the purpose of the health ministry team, ask for ideas from the group, and set a few reasonable goals. Also, find a mutually agreed-upon, regular time for the team to meet that is consistent during the first year of planning and development. Don't worry about having high expectations. At this point, your goal is to get the group started in a positive direction and earn the commitment of others to help you develop the ministry program.

Determine roles.

It is helpful as you organize to designate some roles. Usually in a new group, this is done by consensus, but be sure that those who are either elected or have volunteered are the best fit for the job. You may wish to have at least a chairperson or co-chairs and a secretary. The chairperson will put together the agenda for and run the meetings. The secretary will keep minutes and send emails to the group as needed. The duties associated with various roles may expand and change, so the group should keep note of the expectations for each position and the amount of time various responsibilities may take.

Plan, Plan, Plan

Remember that the initial goals you set at the first meeting should be fluid and dynamic. As time goes on, you may need to add new goals and/or abandon others.

Plan your first activity (see chapters 8 and 9). There are many potential service activities that a health ministry team could facilitate or host. You will need to set priorities, particularly in the first year, so as not to become overwhelmed. Think about your activities as falling into two categories: those that are internal and those that are external. *Internal activities* are those that minister to your own members of the congregation. The *external activities* are outreach ministries to the community and beyond. Try to keep a balance between these two, but your team will need to determine the areas of focus at that first meeting. Here are some examples of internal and external activities:

Internal	External
Assure building safety	Homeless ministry
Childproof the nursery spaces	Food pantry
Blood pressure screening	Prison visitation
Purchase an AED	Soup kitchen
Schedule a health fair at your church	Angel Tree ministry
Sponsor a speaker on a health topic	Pregnancy assistance center

Some groups find it helpful to set the entire calendar for the year in advance. However, don't try to do this at the first meeting. Rather, have a person designated to take minutes. After the first meeting, ask the group members to think about other activities to add to the calendar. Then, at subsequent meetings, begin to fill in the calendar. At the beginning, aim for a reasonable goal, like one activity per month, or one per quarter.

Get Started

Begin by informing the congregation about the presence and purpose of the health ministry team. Then start with small, less demanding, reasonable activities. Be visible and available. Choose activities that do not require as many resources to get started. Start slow and get good workflow, communication, and positive outcomes from your first efforts in order to build the confidence of the team and the confidence of the members of the congregation *in* the team. You can move on to more challenging activities later.

Perhaps you want your first activity to be an internal one where the team examines the safety of the environment and makes necessary modifications to decrease the risk of injury or harm. Or maybe your goal is to have a rotating schedule for a health professional to be on call during all church services in case of emergencies like the one at Sarah's church at the beginning of this chapter. Outreaches such as health fairs or homeless ministries may take more planning and additional volunteers, so start small and work up.

✔ Are You Health Aware?

- Has your faith community thought about a health ministry?

- What ministries are going on right now that are related to health?

- Who is in charge of these ministries?

- Does anyone in your church show a particular passion and gift related to health awareness? Health ministries?

✔ Health-Aware Checklist

_____ Who might want to be part of your health ministry team?

_____ What are some possible goals and timeline or ministry aspirations?

_____ Whom could you invite to an initial brainstorming session about forming a health ministry team?

_____ What types of internal and external activities are most needed in your congregation? In your community?

_____ What types of activities are you most passionate about?

_____ Which activities are feasible, considering available resources?

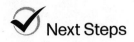 **Next Steps**

Right now we can:

Within three months, we will:

Our end-of-year goal is:

CREATING RISK AWARENESS

"While I was with them,
I protected them and kept them safe."
—John 17:12a

What's Wrong with This Picture?

In the crawler nursery, eighteen-month-old Luke starts toward the toy box on all fours. A cabinet distracts him, and he crawls over to investigate. After a few tries, he opens the cabinet and grabs a brightly colored spray bottle.

"Oh no, Luke, not the cabinet again! Let's go play with the toys." The nursery worker replaces the bleach spray and carries Luke to the toys.

If you have identified risks such as missing safety locks on cabinets, storing dangerous chemicals within a child's reach, and not addressing the problem the first time it happened, then you are safety aware. Is your church putting safety first?

Safety first is an important goal for any group. Identifying safety and health risks is a key step toward promoting health. The information in this chapter will guide you in establishing ways to reduce risk, treat emergencies, and improve health for all ages.

Nursery Safety

The nursery is one of the first places where young parents make a decision about your church. Create a safe place for babies and children. Not only is it our moral obligation to protect the vulnerable, it is also our responsibility to help parents feel secure knowing that their little ones will be cared for by qualified people while they are worshiping or ministering elsewhere.

Teach volunteers about basic child development.

All volunteers need to understand how children within their care learn and develop. For example, knowing that infants and toddlers learn about the world by putting things in their mouths is important. Volunteers armed with that knowledge can avoid planning crafts or activities with small parts that could present a choking hazard. You might be surprised that this isn't common knowledge. Table 7.1 at the end of this chapter provides a quick summary of normal child development and suggestions that all workers should know.

Recruit adequate helpers.

Maintain a safe ratio between volunteers and children. The National Association for the Education of Young Children recommends the following ratios:

- Infants (birth–15 months)—1:3 for a group of 6 and 1:4 for a group of 8.
- Toddlers (12–28 months)—1:3 for a group of 6 and 1:4 for a group of 8 to 12.
- Toddlers (21–36 months)—1:4 for a group of 8; 1:5 for a group of 10; 1:6 for a group of 12.[1]

What is your typical ratio of workers to children? Does it meet national standards?

Criminal background checks for all who work with children are a must. Follow an application process to be sure workers meet your standards. There should always be a minimum of two adults in any classroom. Make no exceptions.

Next, look carefully at the nursery environment. Imagine you are an infant or toddler. Get down on their level. What safety hazards do you see? Look for any potential dangers, such as uncovered outlets, toys with small pieces, toys that are broken, cabinets or doors that could pinch little fingers, any sharp objects or edges, or blinds with strings that hang down. All nurseries should have basic essentials, such as access to a tall sink that is for adults only, a changing table that is in the main part of the room and in full view of others, swings and cribs that have child-safety features and meet accepted standards, high cabinets to hold supplies, and childproof locks on all other drawers or cabinets. All cleaning materials must be stored well out of reach. A nursery safety checklist is provided in Table 7.2 at the end of this chapter.

Quick Check: How Safe Is Your Nursery?

Hand-washing

- All workers should wash their hands frequently. Hand-washing is the number one way to prevent the spread of germs.

Disinfecting

- Wipe down all surfaces and toys with an approved, germ-preventing solution or with wipes at the end of each care session.
- Use toys that can be cleaned with a bleach solution.
- Launder all linens, blankets, or towels after each use.
- Use disposable items as possible.
- Empty trash after each session.
- Spray the changing table and toilet after each use.
- Have tissues and disposable gloves handy.

Communicate Sick Child Policy

- Make guidelines available for parents. Ask parents of children who are sick or running a fever to keep their child at home to prevent the spread of illness. Report any signs of illness to parents.

Communicate Healthy Volunteer Policy

- Ask volunteers to stay home if they are ill or running a fever.

- Develop a substitute policy and review it often.

Teach parents about childproofing their homes. Provide a strong example by having a safe childcare space in your building. Hand out safety information to parents. If your church has sufficient resources, consider providing daycare services or starting a preschool to help families with two working parents or single mothers who need reliable childcare. Creative leaders can also use their church building to host special events that benefit the greater community as an outreach. Choose an interesting topic and advertise locally.

Ministry Event Suggestions

Car Seat Safety

- Contact your local hospital and invite a nurse to provide a car seat safety class. Attenders can bring their car seats to ensure compliance with safety standards.

First Aid

- Schedule a CPR class through your local American Heart Association or Red Cross. Ask them to teach choking treatment and resuscitation techniques.

Poison Prevention

- Accidental poisoning is a leading cause of injury in the U.S. for children under five. Invite your local police or poison-control officials to talk about poison prevention.

Immunizations

- Ask the county health department to talk about immunizations and their importance.
- Consider offering your church as a site for booster shots.

Offer Parenting Classes

- Use professional counselors, pastors, teachers, or nurses to offer parenting classes or parenting support groups.
- Consider beginning a MOPs (Moms of Preschoolers) program.

Case Study

Mrs. Smith is a kind, elderly servant leader in charge of the art project for the two- and three-year-olds during Vacation Bible School. She has taken great care to collect all the items for a craft that includes small beads, sequins, and white glue. Since these items are inappropriate and pose a potential choking hazard to toddlers and children of this age, how do you handle this situation?

Building Safety

Examine your facilities inside and out to identify potential hazards. Falls are one of the most common causes of accidents for older people, and they often result in fractures or other complications. To minimize the risk of falls, flooring inside and outside should be secure. Avoid bricks or pavers on walkways, opting for smooth cement or asphalt. Use inside flooring that is not slippery. Low-pile mats secured to the floor will help to prevent tripping. Avoid throw rugs in other areas of the building. Make entry ramps available for those who cannot climb stairs. If you live in an area with snow, have a plan in place for clearing walkways and helpers on hand for those who need assistance during inclement weather.

For children's ministries, choose playground equipment and toys that are safe and age-appropriate. Consult a specialist when planning a play area for your church. Safety of materials, height of equipment, and cost considerations are factors that an experienced builder can assist with. Do not accept donated items that do not meet these standards.

Be sure to have enough smoke detectors that are in compliance with the rules of building safety. Place carbon monoxide detectors throughout the building. Change the batteries regularly, following manufacturer instructions.

Consider the unique needs of older adults when planning and assessing building safety. Install handrails and an accessible restroom on the main floor. Seating in the main room where services take place must be accessible to those with wheelchairs and walkers. Aisles should be wide enough to easily accommodate an oversized wheelchair. Of course, all features of the building should meet or exceed safety codes.

Immunizations

The Centers for Disease Control and Prevention recommend that all children be immunized. The list of shots that infants and children are required to have now has grown considerably. Current recommendations can always be found at the CDC website.

Some parents object to immunization on religious grounds. While choosing whether to immunize is a parental right in the United States, congregational leaders should be aware that immunizations are built on the principle of herd immunity. For example, vaccinating children early for polio has virtually eradicated the disease in the United States. But consider what happened in Japan in the 1970s. There were only a few cases of whooping cough due to the good immunization program, but then rumors spread that maybe the pertussis vaccine was not necessary. As a result, parents stopped vaccinating their children, resulting in an epidemic of 13,000 cases with 41 deaths. Vaccinations are a way to help keep diseases at bay and eventually eliminate them. Despite how helpful vaccines are, if parents choose not to vaccinate their children, we should still receive them in our church congregations with love and respect, recognizing the risk to their children and others while doing our best to prevent the spread of infection in the church setting. Have a sick child policy and provide extra education for those working with non-immunized children.

Food Allergies and Special Diets

Food allergies are a common occurrence and can be life-threatening. Ask all parents about any allergies their children may have. Serious food allergies should be noted on the child's diaper bag (if applicable), and/or in the log-in record. With the parents' permission, a note should be placed where childcare workers can see this important information as a reminder.

Quick Tips

- Keep a notebook that logs allergy information about children.
- Have parent contact information in the log so parents can be located quickly in case of emergency.
- Instruct parents to clearly label the diaper bag with a bright note that states any allergies.
- Instruct workers on the use of EpiPens or rescue inhalers. Obtain parental permission in advance to use them in case the parent cannot be located quickly.

The Mayo Clinic lists several common signs of food allergies. These include itching, hives (red blotches on the skin), tingling or swelling of the lips or mouth, nasal congestion, wheezing, dizziness, or fainting. Symptoms may range from mild to extremely serious. The most serious type of food allergy can trigger what is called *anaphylaxis*, a life-threatening emergency. Signs and symptoms can occur within minutes to a few hours after the allergen exposure. A rapid pulse, difficulty breathing, swollen throat (complaint of feeling like the throat is closing), dizziness, and loss of consciousness are serious signs that require emergency treatment. Call 911 if these symptoms occur.

Be careful when planning food for group events. Offer good alternatives like sugar-free, low-calorie, gluten-free, lactose-free, or low-carb choices for those of any age who follow a special diet. Label these clearly for buffet or potluck-style meals. In the classroom setting, encourage parents to bring a safe snack for the entire group so that children with food allergies do not feel left out or different from others. If this is not possible, choose snacks for little ones that are usually allergen-free (such as bananas or pretzels), while avoiding common offending foods like peanut products, strawberries, or chocolate. Teenagers can be especially sensitive to being singled out for any reason, so be sure that youth ministry leaders and volunteers are sensitive to these needs when planning outings and parties.

First-Aid Kits

Ideally, you will want to place first-aid kits in different areas of your facility. For example, allocate one to the nursery, one to the sanctuary, and one to the gym. Each of these kits can contain a few additional items appropriate to the particular area near their location. For example, in the kit for the gym you may want to have a finger splint, more bandages and tape, and instant ice packs. In the kit for the sanctuary, smelling salts and an emesis bag might be more appropriate.

When making first-aid kits, use a plastic container that seals securely. Select different colors, sizes, or shapes to distinguish between different kits. Store the kits in a safe place away from children but easily accessible to adults in an emergency.

Table 7.3 gives a list of basic first-aid resources and supplies that you will want in every kit. However, you may design particular first-aid kits for particular places or scenarios. Note that in a personal first-aid kit for the home, you would have over-the-counter ointments and medications like aspirin or Tylenol, antibiotic ointment, hydrocortisone cream, antacids, and anti-itching lotion. However, unless you have a licensed professional coordinating your congregational health program, it is best not to keep these medications in a public first-aid kit. Some people may be allergic to certain medications, which could make their condition worse. Small children could get into the kit and ingest something they shouldn't. It is not the responsibility of church workers to give medicine to others. Planning ahead for emergencies can make it easier for everyone involved and can provide the comfort to the injured that we seek to give as a caring, Christian community.

AED (Automatic External Defibrillator)

You may have noticed that many public buildings, including airports, libraries, and stores, have an AED that trained personnel can use to deliver a shock to a person's heart in the event of a heart attack. Many churches choose to have an AED available on the wall in a central location. If your facility elects to do this, one person (preferably a licensed healthcare professional) should be in charge of checking and maintaining the device. Only those trained and certified in CPR and the specific use of the AED should use this device in an emergency. It is also a good idea to have a blood pressure cuff, stethoscope, and gloves, as well as a ventilator mask or other protection right next to the AED so that trained nurses or physicians in the congregation can use these items if needed to attempt resuscitation. While an event necessitating the use of an AED can be scary, having the equipment available can mean the difference between life and death while waiting for emergency personnel to arrive.

Handling Emergencies

Even when taking steps to reduce risk, you will sometimes need to know some basic first aid. Accidents happen in the nursery, such as bumps, bruises, or bites, and sometimes more serious situations occur, such as choking. Remember that the first principle is to reduce the risk of harm by taking preventive steps as discussed early in this chapter. Always call for emergency medical help when in doubt. It is better to err on the side of caution than to take no action.

This section will give you some basic first-aid tips for common emergencies.

Basic Guidelines for All Common Emergencies

- Prevention is best, so think safety first.
- Notify the family and describe how the injury happened.
- If you have any doubt about how bad the injury is, encourage the person to seek medical attention.
- Know where your emergency kit is and keep it stocked.

Bites

Bites caused by another child in the nursery are relatively common and usually not an emergency. However, bites that cause bleeding or bites from insects or animals may be more serious. Follow these general guidelines:

- Wash the area with soap and warm water.
- Inform parents of what happened.
- Urge parents to seek medical care from their physician for animal bites.
- For spider or snakebites, write down a description of the animal or insect and call your local Poison Control Center for further instructions. Keep the affected person (and their parents, if applicable) still and calm. If the bite is on an arm or leg, keep the limb *below* the level of the heart.

Possible Broken Bone

When someone falls and you can see obvious deformity of the injured body part, treat it as a broken bone. While it may become swollen and discolored, other times there may be no outward signs except pain and difficulty moving. Seek medical help in all cases except the obviously minor ones. X-rays or CT scans are the only definitive way to confirm damage to a bone. Always notify parents or family members and describe how the accident happened. Do not move the injured part. Provide comfort and reassurance to the injured person while waiting for treatment or emergency personnel to arrive. When the injury involves the neck or back, do not move the person at all.

Bruises

Check the size of the bruise and note the cause. Small bruises are generally non-emergencies. Apply a cool cloth for fifteen minutes to decrease swelling and pain. Large bruises with lots of swelling and pain can indicate underlying damage and may need to be seen by a professional healthcare provider.

Burns

Burns can be very serious and painful. Use good safety practices to prevent burns, especially around campfires and when roasting hot dogs or marshmallows. Do not allow children to play around fires. Teach the words STOP, DROP, and ROLL.

- For small burns that leave a red spot, place the burned area in cool water for fifteen minutes.
- For large, more severe burns, call an ambulance.
- *Do not* break blisters from a burn because doing so can introduce infection.
- *Do not* use ice directly on the area because doing so can further damage the skin.
- *Do not* put Vaseline, oils, or butter on burns because doing so seals in the heat and can make the burn worse.

Choking

If a person chokes on food or an object and is unable to breathe, cough, or talk, call an ambulance immediately. Encourage coughing because strong coughing can often dislodge the material. If the person choking is conscious, is holding a hand to their throat (the universal distress sign for choking), and is unable to speak, you may be able to help by using abdominal thrusts (also known as the Heimlich maneuver). Follow these steps:

- Go behind the choking person with that person standing up.
- Put your arms around the waist at the height of the belly button and make a fist with one hand, tucking in your thumb, with the other hand over it.
- Press your hands in and upward with moderate force to try to expel the object.
- For children less than one year old, place them face down on the length of your arm and deliver back blows between the shoulder blades to try to expel the object.
- If the person falls unconscious, a person trained in CPR can use their skills to help while waiting for the ambulance to arrive.

Cuts

Most cuts in the church setting will be minor and easily handled by laypeople. However, some cuts can be serious, especially if they happen while people are using dangerous tools, such as during a building project.

- For minor cuts, place a clean cloth, clean paper towels, or clothing over the wound. Apply firm pressure with your hands. Wash the area with soap and water and apply a bandage from your first-aid kit.
- If a cut is spurting blood, an artery may have been damaged. Call an ambulance and keep constant, direct, firm pressure on the wound.

- In serious cases (when bleeding does not stop), continue to apply firm pressure until medical help arrives.

Fainting

Reasons that a person might faint (or pass out) in a congregational setting include:

- Prolonged exposure to heat
- Not eating or drinking for a long period of time
- Standing too long in one place or with locked knees (such as during a choir performance)
- Side effects from medication
- Heart or blood pressure problems
- Early pregnancy

If a person feels faint:

- Ask them to lie down and elevate their legs; protect the privacy of women in dresses or skirts.
- Place their legs on a pillow or chair above the level of the heart to promote better blood flow to the brain.
- *Do not* give the person anything to eat or drink if there is a loss of consciousness.
- Call for emergency assistance if the person does not wake up right away.
- Use smelling salts from your emergency kit to rouse a person who has fainted.

Nosebleeds

Most nosebleeds can be handled by church staff. Causes can include injury, dryness, or other reasons. To treat a nosebleed:

- Ask the person to sit down and lean forward, holding a cloth or tissue on the nose.
- Squeeze the outside of the nostrils firmly right below the bridge of the nose between the thumb and first finger, applying steady pressure for about ten minutes.

- The person should not blow his or her nose right after the nosebleed because this can worsen the condition.
- Although most nosebleeds will stop with this treatment, medical help should be sought if the bleeding is very heavy or continues for a long time.

Poisoning

Most poisonings are preventable. To prevent poisoning:

- Keep all chemicals, cleaning supplies, or toxins out of reach of children.
- Place "icky" stickers on containers to remind people that this is not something to eat or drink.
- *Do not* buy cleaning, chemical, or otherwise poisonous products that look like common children's drinks or food.

To treat suspected poisoning:

- Call the Poison Control Center. Make sure this phone number is in your emergency kit, by every phone in the building, and in the cell phone contacts of every person on your health ministry team.
- Answer the questions from Poison Control professionals and follow their instructions.
- Call an ambulance if the person has trouble breathing, has seizures, becomes unconscious, or has any other abnormal symptoms.
- Most poisonings require a trip to the emergency room for special treatment. Always take the bottle containing the poison with you to the ER.

Puncture Wounds

Most puncture wounds are minor and can be handled by church staff. For example, if a person steps on a tack, this is generally considered to be a minor situation. However, stepping on a rusty nail would require medical attention.

- Cleanse the wound with soap and water.

- Remove the object if it is small.
- If it is large or embedded, do not remove the object yourself. Seek medical help immediately.
- Puncture wounds sometimes cause tetanus, a serious illness that can lead to death if untreated.
- Remind the person to check the date of their last tetanus shot.
- Always notify the parents if a child has suffered a puncture wound.

Stings

Insect stings are common. For most people they are not a serious problem. A small amount of redness, swelling, and pain at the site of the sting are normal and to be expected. However, some people are allergic to insects like bees, and for them a sting can be life-threatening.

- Danger signs after a sting include hives (red, itchy bumps on the skin), trouble breathing, swelling tongue, or difficulty swallowing. Consider this a medical emergency and call an ambulance.
- If the person has an EpiPen, help them give the injection in the outer thigh muscle, if needed.
- Even after effective use of an EpiPen, a person should still seek medical attention.

Dental Accidents

Sometimes teeth get knocked out during sports or other accidents. If this happens:

- Save the tooth and place it in a Ziploc baggie in clean water or milk.
- The person should get medical and/or dental attention right away, particularly in the case of permanent teeth being knocked out.

- When a child loses a baby tooth (regardless of whether it was already loose), rinse out the mouth with water. Save the tooth in a baggie and tell the parents what happened.

Trouble Breathing

A person who has trouble breathing may be in serious trouble, but you can help. Breathing problems have a variety of causes including choking, asthma, allergies, heart conditions, respiratory conditions, or exposure to toxins. First, try to determine the cause, and then take appropriate action:

- If the person has a history of asthma, treat it as an emergency and call an ambulance. If the person has a rescue inhaler, help them use it.
- If the person got their breath knocked out while playing sports, wait a few minutes to see if they recover.
- An older person might have heart problems. Ask if it is usual. If they say it isn't, seek medical attention.
- If the person appears to be choking, take immediate steps as described above in the section on choking.

Some facilities have adopted special policies, such as a no-perfume policy if they have members who react with breathing problems to strong odors such as perfumes, hairsprays, cologne, or air fresheners. This is a good way to avoid triggers for those with special sensitivities and helps us follow the Golden Rule of doing unto others as we want them to do unto us.

Planning Age-appropriate Activities

Train your workers and helpers to plan age-appropriate activities and events. See Table 7.1 at the end of this chapter for some general guidelines. Adults have different learning styles and objectives than children or teenagers. Be sure to consider the audience when planning your events. Avoid negative incidents or feedback by planning the right activities for the right age groups.

Mary is in charge of planning the activity for the first and second graders during Sunday school. She is having trouble finding an age-appropriate game for them to play. What would you suggest to her?

Share a Safe Welcome

By following these simple guidelines, you can make your place of worship a safe and friendly environment that is welcoming to all. As Matthew 7:12 states, "do to others what you would have them do to you." When you plan appropriate activities and have emergency plans in place, you are demonstrating care and concern for others and good stewardship of your resources. Evaluate your safety savviness and set appropriate goals. Welcome people more confidently because you know your church is a safe place to enjoy worship, learning, and community.

Are You Health Aware?

- What is the most important safety issue you need to address in your church?

- Who has authority in this area and can authorize a change in practice?

- What is one safety feature that you can improve in your building or environment today?

Health-Aware Checklist

_____ Does the worker-to-child ratio match the national standards?

_____ Have you conducted a safe-room evaluation?

_____ Does your equipment (cribs, swings, toys, etc.) meet approved safety standards?

_____ Are your entrances, hallways, and bathrooms barrier free?

_____ Do you keep up-to-date information about food allergies and communicate it effectively to your volunteers?

_____ Do you have adequate first-aid kits throughout your building?

_____ Do volunteers know where the closest first-aid kit is located?

_____ Do workers know where the AED is located?

_____ Do volunteers know whom to contact in case of an onsite emergency?

 **Next Steps**

Right now we can:

Within three months, we will:

Our end-of-year goal is:

Table 7.1   Normal Growth and Development with Strategies

Age	Major Traits	Helpful Hints
Newborns (birth–12 months)	Learn to cuddle about 2–4 weeks; smiling, laughing and cooing 2–6 months; teething begins about 6 months; can pull to standing by 9 months; may have fear of strangers at 9 months	Comfort by rocking, soothing talk, soft music; avoid toys or objects with small parts; safety and protection from harm are essential; require complete care
Toddlers (12 months–2 years)	Start to walk about 12 months; words develop from one to several; name body parts; learn to do small activities such as brushing teeth, feeding self; beginning potty-training; unsteady with early walking and tend to fall frequently	Have toilet facilities available for those who are potty-training; allow for bathroom breaks; avoid crafts or activities with small pieces; singing and music are appropriate; have large, safe toys for play; avoid crafts that include small items such as buttons, sequins, small rocks, coins, or pins; be sure to provide adequate adult supervision for toddlers
Preschoolers/early childhood (3–5 years)	Learn to share and play with others; have all 20 teeth; potty-trained; begin to draw and use safe scissors; balance is stable; can catch a ball and skip	Change activities frequently to keep attention; keep stories short; use pictures, hands-on activities, and music or videos; plan outdoor activities in good weather; encourage cooperative play and sharing

Age	Major Traits	Helpful Hints
Grade-school age/middle childhood (6–12 years)	Ages 6–7 can understand and speak clearly; play games with rules; ages 8–9 have better gross motor and increased coordination, have a 2,000-word vocabulary, make friends of same gender, are becoming more independent; ages 10–12 may experience growth spurts and awkwardness, have a 4,000-word vocabulary, want to be included in the group; notice those of opposite gender	Group activities that include role-playing and teams are appropriate; can listen to longer presentations; remember that middle school is a time of awkwardness and body changes; help kids this age to feel successful and included in the group; be aware of potential bullying and take steps to prevent; this age group benefits from inclusion in church ministry opportunities such as puppets, worship team, music, or attending camp
Early teens/adolescence (13–18 years)	Growth spurts, puberty; relationships with peers become more important; tension with other family members is common	Strong peer relationships and role modeling from youth leaders are important; youth in this age group appreciate special events (such as retreats, trips to amusement parks, outings, concerts, other activities) with their church leadership
Late adolescence (18–21 years)	Physical growth is complete; language fully developed; increased involvement in community; more long-term relationships; self-concept linked to body image	Singles' groups for those in college and careers are popular; activities should be geared toward young adults and their unique needs related to decision-making and integrity

Age	Major Traits	Helpful Hints
Young adults (21–34 years)	Establishing intimate relationships and long-term commitments; making life decisions; may be starting a family; making career decisions	Singles' groups continue to be important for those not in long-term relationships; for those who are, family events, good childcare and instruction in church, and support for the family are essential
Middle-aged adults (35–64 years)	Signs of aging begin; relationship with one's own aging parents is a focus; personal integrity dominant; involved in career, social, professional, volunteer, and civic positions; give back to community through volunteering for meaningful causes; may become grandparents and help care for grandchildren	Building a strong family unit and helping children develop into responsible and happy adults is key in this age group; toward the end of middle adult years, marriage retreat to rediscover and renew relationship with spouse is helpful; involve this group in leadership within the church, but be careful not to overwhelm those with young families
Older adults (65 years and older)	Increase in chronic problems and illness; normal aging changes abound; generally have positive self-concept and are stable, interested in life, find meaning in pleasurable activities; increase in cognitive and sensory issues such as hardness of hearing and increase in the incidence of dementia	Safety of the church environment and fall prevention are important; offering social events, support, and community for older adults may help promote health. For those who develop frailty and illness, a visitation program, recording of worship services, and helping them to remain connected to the church are excellent ministries

Table 7.2

How to Promote Child Safety in Church

_____ Have a clear and organized sign-in and sign-out procedure.

_____ Keep a log to communicate significant events to parents (such as biting or falls).

_____ Release children to parents or parent-designated person and not to other siblings.

_____ Identify an adult security person to patrol the halls during every service to ensure facility and child protection.

_____ Label all diaper bags and personal items.

_____ Have a designated space for each child's items that is out of the reach of children.

_____ Maintain a proper adult-to-children ratio.

_____ Complete background checks, screenings, and references on all workers.

_____ Develop a formal orientation process for all workers and helpers.

_____ Install child protection devices in all rooms (outlet covers, cabinet protectors, etc.).

_____ Identify medical personnel in the congregation who are willing to help in the event of an emergency.

_____ Check all rooms for toys that could present choking hazards and remove them.

_____ Clean all rooms and toys weekly.

_____ Launder all linens after each care session.

_____ Wipe all counters and sinks with disinfectant after each care session.

_____ Instruct all workers about frequent handwashing techniques and ensure they use them.

_____ If outside space is used, be sure it is fenced in, away from traffic, and only has safety-approved play equipment.

_____ Have regular meetings with leadership and helpers to communicate important safety information.

_____ Store all equipment in childproof or locked cabinets.

_____ Regularly inspect cribs, rocking chairs, swings, and other equipment for proper working order and any loose or broken pieces.

_____ Supervise restroom breaks by always having two adults accompany children (if this is not possible, have a bathroom connected to the nursery with a screen for privacy, but always leave the door open).

_____ Adopt a specific checklist for equipment.

Table 7.3

Basic First-Aid Kit Supplies

- Important phone numbers
  - Ambulance
  - Fire Department
  - Police Department
  - Poison Control
- Flashlight and/or penlight
- Tweezers
- Small, sharp scissors
- Smelling salts
- Bandages and pads of various sizes
- Medical tape
- Elastic (Ace) bandages
- Finger splint
- Instant ice packs
- Disposable gloves
- Empty squeeze bottle and/or bottled water
- Clean washcloths in baggies
- Sealable baggies
- Cotton balls
- Ipecac syrup (the only essential medication in your kit, used *only* to cause vomiting after ingestion of a poison and *only* when directed by the Poison Control Center)

8

FOSTERING WELLNESS WITHIN YOUR FAITH COMMUNITY

"Do you not know that your bodies are temples of the Holy Spirit, who is in you, whom you have received from God? You are not your own; you were bought at a price. Therefore honor God with your bodies."
—*1 Corinthians 6:19–20*

Have you ever noticed how often the conversations among members talking after the church service center on health concerns? Harry is discussing with Bill his latest trip to the urgent care clinic, while Jenna is sharing with Ella and Carrie the hot new tip for losing a few pounds. This should really not come as any surprise since most people place a high value on personal health and the absence of disease. As the above scripture suggests, God is within us, and we need to use our bodies to his glory. It follows, then, that we can use our places of worship as centers for promoting wellness through sharing vital information about health and the prevention of illness.

Health Screenings

Screenings can help identify potential health concerns early so you can get the proper treatment from a healthcare professional. Health screenings are a first step toward identifying a health concern or risk, often before you even experience any signs or symptoms of illness. The good news is that, after identifying a potential concern, you can follow up with your primary healthcare provider with the goal of minimizing the damage to your body. Alternately, health screenings can help you feel more confident about your health at any given time when the results are negative.

For the youngest members of the church community, it is best for healthcare professionals to screen for health concerns and developmental issues. The health ministry can help parents of infants, children, and adolescents by inviting a pediatrician, pediatric nurse practitioner, or other professional who specializes in treating children to lead a session explaining the various recommendations, why they are important, and how to access testing and treatment in your community.

When it comes to health screening for adults and seniors in your congregation, it is helpful to think about the screenings you might provide within your church and those that would require the services of a healthcare professional. By informing members of the recommendations of key screenings, you can assist them in making good decisions in caring for their health. In any case, once a health concern is identified for a person in your church, it is critical that you recommend that they seek professional evaluation and treatment. Again, it is helpful to have a list of care providers in the community who specialize in a broad range of physical, mental, and emotional health issues.

The U.S. Department of Health and Human Services offers an outstanding website dedicated to helping you learn how to "live well" at https://healthfinder.gov/myhealthfinder. This easy-to-use site will customize the preventive services recommendations for each person based on age and gender. It will also highlight additional testing based on your family and personal health history. While your health ministry cannot provide many of the recommended screenings, you could help your members prepare a personalized list of recommended services, help explain why these tests are important for their health, and help them connect with the services in your community. The tables that follow in this chapter provide a guide for the most commonly recommended health screenings for the general population as well as specific screenings for men or women.

One health screening that your ministry could offer on a routine schedule is blood pressure monitoring. It is possible to purchase a reliable, automatic cuff-style upper arm monitor at most retail pharmacies. The accuracy of the device should be checked initially against a professional monitor used in a healthcare provider's office and then at least once annually. It is important that the cuff fit the upper arm correctly, so you will need different cuff sizes to meet the various needs of your members.

Having a healthcare professional available when checking blood pressure readings is recommended. If there is an issue such as a high reading, they can then advise the church member on next steps. Recognize that one high reading may indicate that further evaluation is needed but is not necessarily indicative of high blood pressure (also known as hypertension). Many factors can contribute to a high blood pressure reading. When doing the blood pressure checks, members should be relatively still for thirty minutes prior to the reading and should not consume a caffeinated beverage or smoke within that time frame. The person should sit with their feet flat on the floor with the arm resting at the level of the heart on a flat surface like a table. When taking the blood pressure, follow the directions provided by the manufacturer of the device.

A normal blood pressure reading is a systolic (upper number) under 120 mm Hg and a diastolic (lower number) under 80 mm Hg. A systolic reading between 120–139 mm Hg or a diastolic reading between 80–89 mm Hg is considered prehypertension, while numbers above 140 mm Hg systolic or 90 mm Hg diastolic are indicative of hypertension. If the systolic is 180 mm Hg or above or the diastolic is 110 mm Hg or above, this is a critical situation called hypertensive crisis, and emergency care is required. While offering blood pressure monitoring at church can be a wonderful service, remember that it is essential you use the information to encourage members to seek medical care to address any underlying health issues.

Recommended Health Screenings for Men and Women[1,2]

Blood Pressure

Check at least every two (2) years; high blood pressure is associated with heart attacks, strokes, heart failure, kidney issues, and eye problems.

Colorectal Cancer

Check between ages 50 and 75 (earlier if positive family history) and as recommended after age 75; stool test or colonoscopy.

Depression

Feeling down or hopeless, loss of interest in activities for two weeks or more can be signs of depression.

Diabetes

Anyone who has high blood pressure (HBP) or who has been treated for HBP in the past needs to have blood sugar levels tested; diabetes affects the entire body, especially the brain, heart, nerves, feet, and kidneys.

Hearing

Anyone experiencing a change in their hearing ability, typically after age 50, should be assessed by a healthcare professional.

Hepatitis C Virus (HCV)

Advised for those who have injected drugs, those born between 1945 and 1965, and those who received a blood transfusion before 1992; HCV affects the liver and eventually the entire body system.

High Blood Cholesterol

Cholesterol should be checked regularly in anyone who is overweight or obese, uses or has used tobacco, or has a personal or family history of heart disease.

HIV

Those younger than 65 should be screened for HIV, while those over 65 should consult with their health provider.

Lung Cancer

Anyone who smokes or has a history of smoking or a history of exposure to secondhand smoke should talk to their provider about the lung cancer screening. The best advice is to get help to stop smoking.

Overweight & Obese

Being overweight (body mass index [BMI] of greater than 25) or obese (BMI of 30+) can lead to a variety of health issues including diabetes and heart disease. The recommended BMI is 18.5 to 25. Calculating BMI is as easy as doing a Google search ("calculate BMI") and entering your weight and height.

Osteoporosis (bone thinning)

If a person is already known to be at high risk for fractures or is age 65 or above, the recommended screening for osteoporosis is a low-dose X-ray of the spine and hip called a DEXA scan.

Sexually Transmitted Infections (STIs)

The level of risk should be discussed with a healthcare provider; women who are sexually active under the age of 24 should be screened for chlamydia and gonorrhea. STIs can affect a woman's ability to become pregnant and can also affect the baby if a woman is pregnant.

Vision

A basic screening for vision will only indicate if a potential problem exists. If a problem is found, patients will be directed to see a specialist, such as an ophthalmologist or optician for thorough assessment, diagnosis, and treatment.

Recommended Health Screenings for Women[3]

Mammogram

Women should discuss when to begin this screening, as well as its recommended frequency, with their care provider. Those with a family history of breast or peritoneal (womb) cancer may be advised to check for the presence of BRCA1 and BRCA2 genes through genetic testing.

Cervical Cancer

Up to age 65, the Pap smear is recommended every three (3) years, or every five (5) years if Pap smear and human papilloma virus (HPV) screening are combined; women should discuss with their healthcare provider the need for this screening past the age of 65.

Recommended Health Screenings for Men[4]

Abdominal Aortic Aneurysm (AAA)

The abdominal aorta is the body's largest artery, and if it bursts, it can cause serious bleeding and even death. Screening (a painless procedure done via ultrasound) is recommended once between ages 65 and 75 for those who smoked.

Prostate Cancer

Men should discuss with their healthcare provider their level of risk to determine if this screening is recommended. A prostate-specific antigen (PSA) test is typically ordered, which is measured from a blood draw. A digital rectal exam (DRE) to assess the size and to note any irregularities of the prostate is usually completed at this time.

Immunizations

A quick note about routine vaccinations and the need for an annual flu shot is in order. Vaccines protect people from being infected from certain diseases that used to be more common; vaccines also help stop the spread of disease. It is important for everyone to participate. There are some instances when certain vaccines may not be given, especially if it is suspected that an allergy to the vaccine may exist. The decision not to vaccinate should be done in consultation with a healthcare provider.

The CDC provides easy-to-read schedules for immunizations across the lifespan from birth to advanced age. Updated regularly, you can find this information at their website (www.cdc.gov). Infants through teens usually receive their immunizations at an annual visit to the pediatrician or primary healthcare provider. If a child is uninsured or underinsured, the U.S. Department of Health and Human Services offers the Vaccines for Children (VFC) program, providing no-cost or low-cost vaccines. More information can be found at the CDC website.

Within your church's health ministry, you can provide information about the importance of vaccines, immunization schedules, and resources about where to access vaccines in your community. Another way to support your members is to offer a flu-shot clinic. Each year around October, the flu shot becomes available that will best protect against the flu viruses suspected for any given year. It is important to be vaccinated yearly because immunity to the various flu viruses decreases, and the viruses are continually developing new strains. Though readily available throughout the healthcare community, it is possible to set up a flu clinic at your church. You would need to partner with a pharmacy or other source for the vaccine and use the services of a healthcare professional to administer the vaccine. You might tap into the professional members of your healthcare ministry. While this may be too ambitious for most churches, it could provide a valuable and convenient service to your members. You might even see more members at worship during flu season and know that you helped make that possible.

Healthy Lifestyle Classes

The choices we make related to what we eat, drink, or smoke, how many hours we sleep, and how active we are on a daily basis impact our general level of health and well-being in a significant way. Lifestyle changes—even small ones—can have a big impact on our health and can even play a role in improving health with a chronic condition. This is an area where the church ministry can flourish. While it is beyond the scope of this book to cover all lifestyle changes in great detail, this section highlights some of the most common areas where people struggle and could use some support to make change happen.

Fitness

Getting and staying active can make a big difference in how one feels physically, mentally, and spiritually. The Department of Health and Human Services recommends that healthy adults include aerobic exercise and strength training in their fitness plans, specifically:

- At least 150 minutes of moderate aerobic activity or 75 minutes of vigorous aerobic activity a week
- Strength-training exercises at least twice a week[5]

Older adults are encouraged to be as active as possible if 150 minutes becomes beyond their capability, and a focus on activities that promote balance—such as tai chi or yoga—is highly encouraged. At the other end of the age continuum, children and adolescents should engage in at least 60 minutes of activity including aerobic, bone-strengthening, and muscle-strengthening physical activities that are age appropriate.

The possibilities of supporting healthy changes in physical activity within the church are limitless as you can create fitness opportunities for all age groups. Always remind members to check with their healthcare provider before beginning a fitness program, especially if they have preexisting conditions. The next section offers just a few ideas. What are some fresh ways to get your members moving?

Physical Activities a Church Health Ministry Could Facilitate

Senior Walking Group

The church building can be a great place to meet for a starting point. Or identify a park, shopping mall, or public walking area in which to gather. Set up a schedule so this can be a regular practice. Large congregations can have numerous offerings.

Parent Stroller Group

Wrap the babies up and get walking. This activity also provides a social opportunity for parents.

Running or Biking Group

For those who like to set a faster pace and push harder, this group could provide support to keep everyone on track and advancing.

Light Weight-training Group

Use the space in the church building for members to stretch and bring their light weights. Whether using group exercise or working individually, this is a great way to stay motivated.

Yoga and/or Tai Chi

These disciplines are great for strengthening the core and improving balance. See if you have anyone with expertise to lead the groups, or sign up for online videos. These are often free or low cost.

Sports Leagues

Softball, baseball, volleyball, bowling, or golf are some of the possibilities. These can be developed by age group or gender, or they can simply include all who are interested, depending on your context. Teams can complete with other faith-based groups for added fun.

Nutrition and Weight Management

Let's start this discussion by avoiding the D-word: Diet. Dieting has so much emotional baggage associated with it that it is better to focus on what is really important, which is healthy eating. Healthy eating simply means eating food that is nutritious, in the right proportions, and in the right balance. Healthy can be exceptionally difficult in a world that seems to super-size every food and drink choice while producing over-processed foods containing high-fructose corn syrup, too much sodium, and unhealthy fats. So where does one begin?

A great place to start is at the United States Department of Agriculture's free website: www.choosemyplate.gov. MyPlate focuses on eating healthy through choosing the right portions of food from fruits, vegetables, protein foods, grains, and dairy. The site provides information about saturated fat, sugar, and sodium with suggestions on how to reduce the intake of these substances. There is specific information across all age groups and in many different languages. There are pages devoted to physical activity, menus, recipes, food safety, and eating on a budget. One area that is updated regularly focuses on online tools, including SuperTracker, which can be set up to allow groups (like your church) to work together toward healthy eating and physical activity goals.

By using MyPlate as the foundation for your classes, you can work through each of the topic areas over the established schedule of your group. Members can access the site at home or from the public library during the week. You can celebrate together the progress members are making with one small change at a time.

In some communities, finding affordable, healthy foods and beverages may be a challenge. Your church may need to get involved with promoting farmers' markets, creating community gardens, or encouraging full-service markets to locate in under-served areas.

With more than two in three adults considered to be over-weight or obese in the U.S.,[6] a special group might be designed for those who want to lose weight in your congregation. In addition to MyPlate, another option might be establishing a Weight Watchers group at your church. It is important for members to find support in one another as they work on healthier eating, to celebrate to-gether times of success, and to help motivate each other when the challenges seem too great.

Sleep and Rest

Until recently, the importance of sleep has been downplayed in our fast-paced society. In fact, many people boast about how little sleep they need to function each day. Few adults actually sleep the recommended seven or more hours per night, while ado-lescents and children may find it difficult to get the recommended eight to ten hours for teens and twelve or more hours for younger children.

Sleep is a vital part of our health and well-being. Sleep allows the brain to recharge through the night so it is ready to learn and function at its best. Sleep deficiency is associated with difficulty making decisions, inability to control emotions and behavior, and is even related to depression and suicide. Sleep helps our bodies recover from our busy days. A consistent lack of sleep is linked with a variety of physical concerns including heart disease, high blood pressure, stroke, diabetes, and obesity.

As you prepare to start a class on healthy sleeping and rest within the congregation, check out this great website by the National Institutes of Health (NIH): https://www.nhlbi.nih.gov/health-topics/sleep-deprivation-and-deficiency. This site provides information about what happens when we sleep, why sleep is important, the effects of sleep deficiencies, how much sleep is enough, and strategies to promote sleep. While this information could be provided in one class period, there is a benefit to meeting over the course of a month or more. During this time, members can log their sleep patterns and monitor what helps or hinders their sleep. By bringing this information back to the group, all can benefit from the information shared.

A special group that faces challenges with sleep are those who do shift work, such as nurses, doctors, police, and factory workers. Remember that the best time for these members to meet might be during the day.

Stress Management

Stress takes a toll on the body, mind, and spirit. It is estimated that 70 to 85 percent of all visits to primary care providers are related to stress. From backaches, headaches, and upset stomachs to fatigue, lack of energy, restlessness, and everything in between, stress is often the root cause. Stressors like getting a divorce, getting married, being fired, financial instability, building a new house, experiencing a traumatic event, or just everyday small events that add up can result in a stress reaction. Being able to manage the stressors of daily life is an important step toward a healthy life.

The health ministry program can make a difference by creating focused sessions that include identifying stressors, understanding how stress affects the body and the mind, how to recognize the signs and symptoms of stress, and how to manage stress and develop new coping strategies. There are many available resources to assist you in developing your program, but one useful source by HelpGuide can be found here: https://www.helpguide.org/articles/stress/stress-management.htm/.

What Are Some Ways to Manage Stress?

- Living a healthy lifestyle that includes good nutrition and exercise
- Being involved in positive, supportive relationships where effective communication and respectful listening are part of your interactions
- Learn mind-body methods such as:
  - Deep breathing techniques
  - Relaxation exercises
  - Guided imagery
  - Prayer
  - Meditation
  - Yoga
- Start a daily gratitude journal and write at least five things that bring you joy, happiness, or positive feelings
- Laughter
- Increase your own self-awareness to engage in behaviors that stop unwanted behaviors

Depending on the size of your membership, you might want to have stress-management groups for different developmental age groups. The issues confronting young married couples or singles will probably vary significantly from older adults. It is also important to refer members to mental-health experts or even crisis centers if you find that a level of stress is extreme, a person is having difficulty performing daily activities, or there are indicators of self-harm or harm to others.

Health-Education Seminars

As compared to the series of lifestyle classes discussed earlier in this chapter, health-education seminars would be single-session offerings on a variety of health-related topics. There really is no limit to the areas you could explore. What is important is that you select topics that are relevant to your membership. To this end, you might develop a short survey to see what interests the members and follow up with issues with the highest rank. Once the seminar program has started, you can ask participants about future programs of interest.

Health-education seminars are a great way to engage the healthcare professionals and other members of your congregation with expertise to share their knowledge without needing them to commit to a longer program. Lasting about ninety minutes, these seminars would include an introduction to the health topic and key considerations related to the topic. It is important to share national or community resources with participants so they have the information to continue following up. Always provide time for questions and answers within the session since this is when some of the key opportunities for learning and sharing occur. It is likely that some of the seminars may result in additional sessions or even the request for a support group. Assuming that the resources exist within the congregation, this could be a valuable service of the health ministry program. The following list provides some common topic ideas with a helpful, nationally recognized resource that might be useful as you begin a health-education program in your congregation.

Topic Ideas and Suggested Resources

- Dementia and Alzheimer's Disease: Alzheimer's Association (www.alz.org).
- Heart Disease: American Heart Association (www.heart.org).
- Depression: National Institute of Mental Health (www.nimh.nih.gov).
- Substance Abuse: Substance Abuse and Mental Health Services Administration (www.samhsa.gov).

- Choosing a Nursing Home: AARP (www.aarp.org).
- Hospice and Palliative Care and Advance Directives: National Hospice and Palliative Care Organization (www. caringinfo.org).

There are so many important topics and concerns related to health promotion, disease prevention, and wellness that it is easy for even the most motivated church to become overwhelmed. The best way is to begin small, with one or two ideas that will help your members move toward a healthier lifestyle. There will be time to build your program as more members experience the benefits of being part of a church that focuses on their health and well-being.

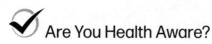 **Are You Health Aware?**

- What is the most important lifestyle issue you need to address in your church?

- Do you know what health-education seminars might be most useful to your members?

- Are there members of your church with expertise in health and wellness topics who would be willing to share their gifts?

 **Next Steps**

Right now we can:

Within three months, we will:

Our end-of-year goal is:

9

REACHING BEYOND YOUR FAITH COMMUNITY

"For I was hungry and you gave me something to eat,
I was thirsty and you gave me something to drink,
I was a stranger and you invited me in, I needed
clothes and you clothed me, I was sick and you looked
after me, I was in prison and you came to visit me.
Whatever you did for one of the least of these
brothers and sisters of mine, you did for me."
—Matthew 25:35–36, 40b

Every community has needs that overwhelm the social system, delay the timely delivery of care, and often go unnoticed. Children go to bed hungry. People can't pay their utility bills. Many are homeless. And that is just the identified needy. What about the very hungry, the isolated strangers, the kids with holes in their shoes that you never see, the children who only eat when there is free lunch provided at the public school?

The passage in Matthew 25 gives us much to think about. The righteous person in this passage does not recognize that what was done for hungry, homeless, needy people was done for Jesus. Notice the needs met: food, drink, housing, clothing, healthcare, and visits in prison. How wonderful that many outreach ministries are listed right here in this passage! Note also that these ministries provided help for the "least" of Jesus's brothers and sisters—that is, those who need this help the most. This portion of Scripture represents health awareness at its best. This chapter will give practical tips for establishing outreach ministries, such as:

- food pantries/soup kitchen/meal ministries
- health fairs/screenings
- homeless shelters
- missions
- support groups
- prison ministries

No one can meet all needs. However, each of us can do something.

A Place to Begin

There are numerous ways to reach beyond your congregation to help others. Your health ministry team can advise the larger congregation about potential ministry opportunities. There are a number of factors to consider when choosing where to put valuable time and resources. For example, even if a small group of people in the church have a passion to help the homeless population in your community, the particular ways to serve need to be carefully examined. Think about ways to work with existing resources like providing a food pantry, donating needed items, or serving hot meals at the local relief center. These are more realistic than starting off with housing the homeless in your church building. While offering a homeless shelter is a wonderful goal, it requires a large number of volunteers and significant finances, and involves insurance implications for the buildings and property as well as assessment of potential risk.

Start with small, manageable projects and evaluate success. Know who is already meeting needs in your community and consider joining their efforts. Be willing to learn from each experience, whether positive or negative. Keep track of barriers and how you deal with them.

Always start with prayer, and choose your projects wisely. Then see what specific projects your team members are most passionate about. After identifying some potential areas of outreach, step back and pray, both together and individually. Then come back together as a team to share where the members feel God is leading to begin a new project.

After deciding on a small project to begin with, gain the support and approval for your outreach from the appropriate committees and leadership in your congregation. Before taking your proposal to these groups, be sure to have a concisely written, brief summary about your project (1–2 pages is ideal). Include purpose, hours of commitment, people involved, resources needed, costs, and how you will raise the funds to cover the costs. Be willing to accept the final decision of the church leadership regarding your team's proposal.

Examples of Health-related Outreach Ministries

While there are many health-related ministries to expand your congregation's reach, remember the general tips above when beginning any type of service project. Some suggestions and background information on various outreaches are provided here.

Food Pantries, Soup Kitchens, and Meal Ministries

Food ministries are one of the most common ways to expand your outreach beyond your own borders, perhaps because they directly answer the call "for I was hungry and you gave me something to eat." Nutrition is a basic human need. Before we can address spiritual needs, we must meet basic physical needs. Providing a meal for a lonely, older person or helping put food on the table for a hungry family is also a spiritual ministry, as our Scripture passage has indicated. The simple act of serving a hot lunch to the hungry, as you would to the Lord, is a selfless act that shows love.

These types of ministries may take several forms. You can serve meals at the local shelter or soup kitchen. This is a meaningful family project that can have a lasting impact on teens who serve with their parents, particularly when giving up one's own holiday traditions to help serve a Thanksgiving or Christmas Eve dinner to the needy.

Helping with food delivery to those who cannot get out of their homes is another community service. This might mean volunteering for an organization like Meals on Wheels or organizing and preparing dinners for someone who has recently had surgery.

Some congregations have an annual food drive and make Thanksgiving, Christmas, or Easter baskets for those less fortunate. These baskets generally contain an entire holiday meal, including a turkey or ham, instant potatoes, sweet potatoes, stuffing mix, green beans, rolls, and dessert. If someone in your group has access to a refrigerated truck, essential items such as milk, eggs, and butter can be added to the baskets for delivery.

Finally, food pantries help fill a gap for the homeless or underserved who cannot afford to feed their families. In fact, many homeless persons use local food banks on a regular basis to make ends meet. These types of ministries are a good place to start when considering where to put time and resources for your new health team. Consider the following example:

Jane's new health team discussed possible outreach ministries at their first two meetings. After a time of prayer and contemplation, the group felt strongly that they should begin with addressing problems in a nearby community that had a high rate of poverty and unemployment. The team wanted to begin by opening a food pantry at the church that would be staffed by volunteers twice a week from nine o'clock in the morning until noon. The pastor and church secretary were also present in the building during these hours. They felt it was important for a pastor to be available if more help was needed or if a visitor needed spiritual counseling or guidance. The health team members would be the initial volunteers. They would ask for additional help if the program started to grow.

They identified an available room at the church, and one of the members donated some shelving to store the goods. They were able to get a commitment of regular donations of nonperishable items from one of their adult small groups and three other churches in the area. The youth group stocked the shelves and made up bags of food for a service project.

Jane's team posted flyers about the food pantry in the target community, and a local radio station agreed to advertise it for free. By starting with a smaller project, Jane's team was able to see immediate success by meeting a need in the congregation's own community as they received grateful feedback from those who benefited from this outreach.

Health Fairs and Screenings

Health screenings and/or health fairs are an excellent way to promote wellness in your congregation and the entire community. Nurses typically love to be involved in community outreach in this way. Often, public health departments and other community organizations lack a large physical space to conduct big health fairs. Opening your church facility for this purpose is a wonderful community service.

To start small, consider offering simple screenings before or after church events. These might include blood pressure, stroke, or other screenings that are easy to do. Enlist nurses in the congregation to take blood pressure, or invite student nurses to practice their skills by helping with the screening. Stroke screenings are more time-consuming, but there are excellent tools available that you can use for free, including resources from the National Stroke Association, available online at www.stroke.org. The National Stroke Association also provides free informational fact sheets on a variety of other disorders including atrial fibrillation and heart disease.

A health fair is a good way to get to know others in health organizations in your community. Achieve a successful health fair by planning it well in advance with plenty of volunteers and an active chairperson with a committed committee. A health fair is a perfect project for your parish or faith community nurse to organize, if you have one. Start with the health department and ask what services they could offer to attenders. Partner with a nearby university to have their nursing students help plan and run the fair in collaboration with your health ministry team. Provide specific clinical hours and a site for students to teach with hands-on learning opportunities. Inquire about specialty physicians (such as the local podiatrist, dentist, orthodontist, or a women's health practitioner) in your area to see if they would be willing to set up a table with information and helpful giveaways (toothbrushes, free initial consultations, and the like). Recruit a massage therapist to give five-minute chair massages. Invite your area senior centers, daycare providers, school nurses, and recreational centers to have a table with information or videos for attenders. Consider having breakout information sessions on health topics given by physicians, nurse practitioners, sports medicine experts, or nursing instructors.

You can also focus your health fair on a certain age group, such as seniors or even on a certain topic, such as child safety. Services and information provided will vary depending on the audience. Older adults may benefit more from hearing, vision, stroke, or diabetes screenings. If targeting a younger audience and their parents, consider topics like car seat safety, bike helmets, stranger danger, and good hand-washing.

Homeless Shelters

According to the January 2017 report from the National Alliance to End Homelessness, there are more than 550,000 homeless persons on any given night in the United States.[1] There are multiple causes for homelessness that can include drug addiction, poverty, alcoholism, mental illness, and others. These factors make the important ministry to the homeless complex for the church.

There are numerous ways to help with sheltering the homeless in your community. Some methods require a great deal of resources and time commitment while others are more manageable. Consider the levels of involvement that might be appropriate for your congregation.

Assist Another Church or Community Group

If time and resources are limited, you can partner with another church or community action organization to provide things like gently used clothing, nonperishable food, toiletry items, or bedding. You could also have church members or your team donate their time to help put together blessing bags containing needed items to distribute at the homeless shelter. Some in the church might volunteer to launder the bedding and return it for the next group. Others could help pack lunches for people during the day. Volunteers can help supervise the men's shelter at night (for safety reasons, it might be best for these volunteers to be men, depending on your context and the training each volunteer has). There is always room for volunteers in this kind of outreach ministry. These types of activities require less financial commitment than being in charge of the entire program.

Run a Homeless Shelter in Your Church

If your facilities and health team are large, you might want to consider partnering with local officials to be part of a church rotation to open your gymnasium or fellowship hall for overnight sleeping purposes, or begin such a ministry yourself. To run a year-round shelter as a single church is a daunting, time-consuming effort that carries with it many implications for safety and insurance. It might be better to learn the process by being part of a consortium of churches who partner with a community parent organization that provides instruction, guidance, and oversight in carrying out the ministry. Then, armed with experience, your team may choose to branch out with additional ministry in this area.

James was a member of a rather small church that had a large gymnasium that was seldom used. His pastor asked him to consider heading up a men's homeless shelter ministry in collaboration with a local organization that was recruiting fourteen churches to open their doors one night a week for six months so homeless men could sleep there overnight. The church would have to purchase bedding for between ten and thirty men, provide an evening meal, and offer a light breakfast in the morning. At least two men from the church would have to supervise the group overnight and enforce the rules established by the parent homeless ministry. James felt called to serve in this capacity and organized a rotation of willing men from the church to help. Others in the church also helped by making the evening meal and packing lunches for the homeless men to take with them when they left the next morning.

James found that the ministry was challenging because many of the homeless men in the community had mental illness, a history of substance abuse, or had served time in prison. Even though the parent organization assured the churches that they carefully screened participants in the shelter program and monitored their compliance with counseling and drug testing, sometimes they had to call the police to break up fights. It was a ministry that brought some risk on occasion. Still, James found it rewarding and was able to share the gospel with several men, even helping a couple of them get back on their feet and become independent again.

James learned that this type of ministry required a competent group of strongly committed men from the church after church leadership considered the pros, cons, and cost of undertaking such a ministry.

Missions

Supporting missionaries is a key ministry of many congregations. Some churches allocate a certain percentage of their budget to support both local and international missionaries. Choosing which missions and missionaries to support can be challenging when there are many seeking support and not enough financial resources to support them all. In addition to what your church already does to support missions, a health ministry team can be integrally involved in keeping in touch with your missionaries in various ways, such as:

- writing or emailing regularly
- providing a monthly update from the missionaries to the congregation
- praying for specific needs
- being part of short-term mission trips
- helping run camps that missionaries direct
- donating for specific needs as they become known
- encouraging others to pray and support your missionaries
- making a long-term commitment to support the orphaned or at-risk children identified by your missionaries

While your church may have a separate missionary committee, the health ministry team should collaborate with them, particularly in areas that are related to health and wellness. This may mean the two committees work together on specific projects like raising funds for a new well, water filtration system, proper nutrition, bicycles for missionaries, or a clothing drive for an orphanage. Together, teams can accomplish important work to support those who have dedicated their lives to serve the Lord.

Support Groups

As suggested before, a church usually has unused space during the week that could offer a welcoming place for community members to gather. Support groups for stroke survivors, cancer survivors, alcoholics, families with substance abuse issues, or parents who have lost children may be seeking a neutral place to meet. Donating space for worthwhile causes like these or others is a tremendous community service. In addition, if you have trained, professional counselors in your congregation, asking them to volunteer to either run a group or provide individual or couples' counseling on a limited basis meets a critical need that is present in nearly all communities.

If you are uncertain which types of support groups you feel comfortable using your facilities for, work with your local hospital to determine community needs and how best you can help meet them. Your service may be as simple as providing a space for monthly meetings. Remember to gain support and approval from your leadership before inviting any groups to use your church buildings and grounds.

Prison Ministries

The Prison Policy Initiative estimated that there were more than 2.3 million people incarcerated in 2018 in the U.S., with most of these being in state facilities or local jails.[2] This startling statistic suggests that there is an opportunity in every community for health ministry teams to expand their reach to this vulnerable population and the families that are left at home. Many prisoners receive no visitors, or their visits are confined to irregular video or phone calls. Prison and jail can be lonely places for those who have lost their freedom, regardless of the reason. But these places and periods of confinement also offer time to think and to consider the consequences of past behavior, and they can provide an impetus for change. Prison chaplains bear a heavy responsibility to provide spiritual care for inmates, but local pastors, priests, sisters, and other clergy can share the call to minister to this often forgotten group.

Kairos Prison Ministry is an international organization whose mission is to "share the transforming love and forgiveness of Jesus Christ to impact the hearts and lives of incarcerated men, women, and youth, as well as their families, to become loving and productive citizens of their communities."[3] Founded in 1976, this group has grown to embrace ministry to prisoners across the globe. One of the ways your congregation can engage prison ministry is to partner with and support existing groups like Kairos. Since there is a unique culture in the prison population, supporting those who are experienced in this area is a first step. You can do this by donating money, time, or even baking cookies for their annual party.

Another well-known prison ministry group is the Angel Tree ministry, a program of Prison Fellowship. This organization asks for donations of Christmas gifts for local children whose parents are incarcerated. Local churches receive angel tree ornaments with a child's name and pertinent information such as age, clothing size, and most desired gift. These ornaments are placed on a Christmas tree in the church, and congregation members are asked to take one, purchase gifts, and bring them back to the church for distribution. This is an excellent project for the health ministry team to take on around the holidays. Showing the love of God to complete strangers and bringing joy to their families at Christmas is a unique way to serve the prison population. You can read more about this ministry at www.prisonfellowship.org.

Are You Health Aware?

- What type of ministry does your health ministry team feel most passionate about?

- What small project can you begin first?

- For which of these projects do you already have key people in place who can help and/or have expertise in this area?

- What is a one-year goal for a larger health-related outreach for your team?

 Health-Aware Checklist

Consider this list of smaller and larger projects. Which ones are most feasible for your team to engage?

Smaller Projects	Larger Projects
Blood pressure screenings	Health fair
Volunteer at a food pantry	Establish your own food pantry
Serve at a soup kitchen	Organize and run your own food-related ministry
Donate to a clothing drive	Host your own clothing drive and distribute to the needy
Make sack lunches for homeless individuals	Establish and maintain a homeless shelter ministry
Donate to missions	Organize a short-term mission trip
Share your facility with community groups	Start a specific support group
Donate resources (money or goods) to Kairos Prison Ministry	Volunteer to be a Kairos Prison Ministry visitor
Participate in Angel Tree	Organize an Angel Tree ministry in your church

 Next Steps

Right now we can:

Within three months, we will:

Our end-of-year goal is:

PART THREE

Increasing Your Reach

EMERGING TRENDS
HEALTH AND WELLNESS COACHING AND TECHNOLOGY

"I pray that out of his glorious riches he may strengthen you with power through his Spirit in your inner being."
—Ephesians 3:16

As the evening walking group gathers at the church parking lot, Jenna shouts "6,705!" while Patrick says, "You beat me by over 2,000."

Ella pipes up with "8,442!"

Some strange number game, you ask? Actually, all the members of the group are sharing the number of steps posted on their fitness trackers with the goal of reaching a minimum of 10,000 steps per day. Most will make it after their mile-long walk tonight. At the end of the week, this group will crown a winner for the person who accumulated the most steps. They follow this friendly competition online each day because they are linked as friends in their trackers' app.

Inside the church, Carter, a health and wellness coach, is working with a small group on eating healthier. Each person has finished setting a personal goal for the week; each goal is specific and attainable. When they rejoin the following week, Carter will lead a discussion on how each one did in achieving their goal and exploring what obstacles each faced. Together, they will celebrate their successes and continue to motivate one another to eat nutritious, healthy meals.

Health and Wellness Coaching

Health and wellness coaching is an emerging field that assists individuals in reaching specific goals to improve their health and level of feeling well. Rather than focusing on illness and disease, the emphasis is placed on experiencing an optimal level of function through healthy lifestyle choices. Health and wellness coaches can be that motivating force in identifying and making small lifestyle changes that add up to major gains in one's health.

Your health ministry could tap into using health and wellness coaches to support members in reaching their goals related to reducing stress, improving sleep, eating healthy, and becoming more active. The coaching can take place in groups or individually, onsite at the church or via telephone or videoconferencing. While health and wellness coaches are typically paid for their work, it might be possible that you would find some who would volunteer their services.

Not all who call themselves coaches are equal. You will want to assess whether the coach has completed an extensive training program and achieved certification as a health and wellness coach. With certification, coaches have a level of competence specific to coaching skills, an understanding of the ethics of coaching, and knowledge about health and wellness principles and standards. It is important to find out if a coach has experience working with individuals and groups. Seeking references and asking for testimonials is also a good idea.

Wearable Fitness Devices

As wearable fitness devices have become smaller, smarter, and more reasonably priced, many people embrace the use of such devices as part of their everyday routine. Trackers can provide information about steps, stairs, quantity and quality of sleep, heart rate, and calorie burning. Some interface with scales so you can automatically track your weight changes. There are also applications that can link with these devices and the programs that present the data so you can input what you eat in terms of nutritional value and calories. Most of these devices function in conjunction with smartphones, providing immediate access to significant health-related data.

How does this technology relate to the health-aware church? Because of the popularity of these devices, the church can use the technology to help form activity groups in the congregation. These groups could be organized by age or level of fitness goals. Some members might prefer a walking group, others a running group, and still others a cycling group.

Like the walking group at the beginning of the chapter, groups can come together and track their progress. Many trackers allow participants to link online so each person can see their progress in meeting goals along with others in the group. This helps bond the group and encourages members to send motivational messages or notes of congratulation during the week. In this way, the progress toward a healthier lifestyle brings members closer together outside of the traditional church meeting schedule.

Connecting with Technology

In addition to the trackers, there are numerous downloadable computer and mobile applications available, including many that are free or low cost. For example, MyFitnessPal (www.myfitness-pal.com) allows you to track the foods you eat and count calories. At last review, the application had more than five million foods available in the database, making it easy to identify the calories consumed, whether at home or dining out. This is an area where the younger generation could help the health ministry team stay abreast of new and evolving health applications that can assist members in supporting their health and fitness.

Members might also appreciate assistance in understanding their electronic health records used by most healthcare providers. While this is personal and sensitive information that should not be shared publicly, the health ministry team might offer a class about the use of these records, answer questions about how to access one's records, and discuss how to send a message back to the care provider.

Ways to Stay in Touch with Advances in Technology

- Check in with the younger members of your church; they will often know the hottest new application for fitness.
- Create an ad hoc group of members who love technology to put forward new applications and technology to consider.
- Periodically search the internet using key words like "reviews for new fitness applications," "top new wearable health or fitness devices," or "advances in health technology."
- Host health-education sessions with a community expert on new advances in health technology.

There is no doubt that advances in technology can be both exciting and frustrating. The health ministry can provide a safety net around the evolving digital world so that members can learn how to access and use the many health and wellness devices and applications. Remember that we use technology but depend on the inner strengthening of the Holy Spirit (Eph. 3:16).

 ## Are You Health Aware?

- How could you use health and wellness coaching in your church?

- Is there interest in your church to use wearable tracking devices to promote health? If so, how could you organize these groups?

 ## Next Steps

Right now we can:

Within three months, we will:

Our end-of-year goal is:

11 COLLABORATING AND NETWORKING

"Finally, all of you, be like-minded, be sympathetic, love one another, be compassionate and humble."
—1 Peter 3:8

In order for any congregation to be effective in times of crisis, the church must have already established a collaborative network. To wait until calamity strikes renders the church ineffective and represents a lost opportunity to minister and serve as Jesus would. The wise congregation prepares in advance, is well known for its compassion, and will draw the community closer together in times of distress. Consider what your neighbors in the community would do in a mass crisis. Would they flock to your church for help? Would they welcome your acts of kindness? Do they know who you are?

How should the church respond to crises like terrorism, gang-related violence, natural disasters, and other catastrophes? This chapter provides ideas about how congregations can work with other churches and organizations in the larger community.

Our Part of the Whole

Collaborating and networking outside your own congregation is essential to being a vital member of a community. To expand your reach, you must know about the needs and resources in your own area. What services are available for the poor and needy? What shelters exist for the homeless? What food pantries feed the hungry? What mental health services support the challenged? What centers for pregnancy assistance can you connect with? What hospitals and clinics for the acute and chronically ill should you know about? What emergency services are available? What about counseling and treatment for those with substance abuse issues? Identify what is available and make a list of the gaps in care as well as where your team feels it can best serve. Bathe these discussions and decisions in prayer, seeking God's will for your team.

Work with Other Congregations

A good place to start when increasing your reach through collaboration and networking is to join forces with other congregations who are like-minded. Think about your sister churches or smaller churches than yours who might want to partner in ministry because they don't have the resources that your church does. Maybe you can collaborate on a food pantry or a Christmas musical. Churches with a gymnasium facility have a particular resource that others do not. Sharing your facilities with a smaller church for the purposes of sports activities, Vacation Bible School, or special events like weddings or funeral dinners shows a strong desire for working together. Consider how your health ministry team might reach out to other churches to increase the reach and services of both. It will prepare you to work together in a crisis.

Work with Community Agencies

Most communities have a number of agencies and organizations that need volunteers in order to function. Such agencies usually welcome a congregation's individual members and/or groups to assist in a variety of ways. Put together a list of the agencies in your own community and have your health ministry team prayerfully consider which ones they feel most led to devote time to. The health-aware checklist at the end of this chapter suggests some common agencies in many communities that your group may want to consider connecting with.

Ask for volunteers from your team to contact those chosen from the larger list to see what needs your congregation could fill. Ask how you can collaborate with these agencies and share the love of Christ. For example, a local pregnancy assistance center may have a baby bottle drive each year as a fundraiser. Churches are asked to fill the bottles with change and return them on Mother's Day. The funds go directly to the center to offset costs. Or, invite representatives from chosen agencies to speak at a women's group or Bible study to learn more about how you can partner with them. Each time you donate goods or services to a community agency, you are building your network and extending your reach.

Respond to Crises

One of the times that the church rises to the top in providing service to others is during times of trouble. This could be on a small scale within the community, such as the suicide of a teen at a local high school, when pastors or other professionals in the church volunteer to help with grief counseling. Churches are often called on to help on a much larger scale in the case of mass disasters such as floods, when shelter is needed for victims and families, or in the case of earthquakes with mass casualties, when congregation members volunteer to work with relief teams onsite in other countries.

What each of these examples has in common is the act of Christian caring in which selfless people share themselves and their resources to help others in times of great distress. These are times when people's faith is tested, when nations' leaders turn to God in prayer, and when Christians rise up to provide comfort, food, shelter, medical supplies, and other disaster relief. Maybe more than any other time, the church can be a light of hope to the hurting by being the hands and feet of Jesus to those in need. As John 13:35 says, "By this everyone will know that you are my disciples, if you love one another." Certainly always, but especially in times of trial, the church should show love for all.

Substance Abuse and Addiction

Drug addiction has reached epidemic proportions in many areas of the United States. Addiction is an illness that causes changes in a person's brain, mood, and behavior. The addict doesn't intend to become an addict. For some it happens as a result of prescription drug use for pain. Others give in to peer temptation, try various drugs, and get hooked. You might be surprised at the number of people in your own congregation whose lives have been affected by this problem. Sons and daughters seem to change personalities and no longer care about their family. Parents neglect their children to the point that they lose their parental rights. Grandparents raise grandchildren for parents who cannot break the chains of addiction. One physician called illegal drug use "the scourge of our community."

Mary was a beautiful young woman with a bright future. Her parents were marginal churchgoers. They didn't see the problem coming until Mary was already addicted to heroin. Mary's life spiraled out of control, and her parents couldn't deal with her violent outbursts. They had to ask her to leave home to avoid the negative influence Mary and her friends brought to their younger son.

At the age of eighteen, Mary was living with her boyfriend, who supplied her with drugs. She turned to prostitution to support her habit, became a victim of violence from men who abused her, and was living on the streets when her boyfriend went to jail. Her mother had a nervous breakdown, and her father began drinking to cope with the loss of their precious baby girl. She had become a person they didn't know anymore.

Mary went to prison for her involvement in drug distribution to children at the local school. Her parents had nowhere to turn because nobody in their circle of friends understood the world of drug addiction. They wanted to return to the church they had stopped attending, but they felt they would be judged when people found out about their daughter.

- *How can the local church help people like Mary and her family?*
- *How do you find out about the need?*
- *How can you become the hands and feet of Jesus to a hurting family like this?*
- *How can the church help with the substance abuse problem in the local community?*

  These are difficult questions, but they are logical places to start.

Find Out What Services Your Town Offers

Is there a drug treatment facility? A mental health clinic? Counseling service? Are these facilities for inpatients, outpatients, or both? Is there a nearby mental health hospital that treats those with substance abuse or who are suicidal? Is there a methadone clinic for those trying to kick the heroin habit? Are these services free, or do they require insurance? Does your community have an AA group?

Educate Yourselves

Perhaps someone on your team has a particular interest in, knowledge about, or experience with substance abuse issues. Recruit them to help your team. Learn all you can about the problem in your particular geographic location. The National Institute on Drug Abuse (part of the National Institutes of Health) gives facts on the various types of substance abuse (including specific drugs and alcohol) at: https://easyread.drugabuse.gov.

Identify Gaps in Care

Where is the greatest need? Does that need exist because of lack of funding? Lack of resources? Lack of volunteers? Lack of advocacy? What do the agencies view as the greatest needs? Your health ministry team starts to help by *being aware.*

Be an Advocate

Your health ministry team cannot solve all the world's problems, but you can make a significant impact in certain areas. Before deciding where to delegate resources, blanket all decisions in prayer and gain support from your church leadership. Maybe your community needs a drug treatment center. Or maybe there is a lack of support groups. What can you reasonably do to help? God will bless you for your efforts.

Jesus gave us a wonderful example of loving those who are not in their right minds, who are "not themselves." The story of the man possessed by the demons (named Legion because they were many) shows how Jesus loved the least lovable—the man who had not showered and certainly smelled offensive, who lived among the catacombs, who cut himself with stones and cried out, someone nobody wanted to be around. Yet, in Mark 5:1–20, we see how Jesus cared for this unwanted person by casting out the demons, leaving the man healed, sitting in his right mind, clothed, and wanting to serve the Lord. The people in the town were afraid of him, but Jesus was never afraid. He saw past the ugliness and brokenness of this man and reached out with a caring, healing touch.

We need to do the same. We must look past the hurt and pain and damage brought to a person by drug or alcohol addiction and see the souls of these people who need help, sharing the love and tenderness of Jesus with the most difficult of our brothers and sisters in this world.

Violence and Terrorism

Everywhere we look today, we see frightening examples of violence and terrorism. Lives are lost to gunshots, gang aggression, explosions, suicide bombers, or people turning cars into death machines by driving into a group of innocent bystanders. Both at home and abroad, acts of violence and terrorism should bind us together in support for victims and their families.

Gangs and Violence

Gang-related violence has reached new heights in cities like Chicago, where more than 4,300 shootings were attributed to gang violence in 2016. In 2011, Chicago had a total of 100,000 gang members in 59 gangs, yet only 12,000 police officers.[1] Many of those killed were innocent children caught in the crossfire. And much of the gang violence is related to illegal drug use.

How should the church respond to situations related to gang violence? Certainly supporting those who serve on the police force is one simple way. Are there members of your congregation who are public servants? You can pray for them regularly. But how else can you help? Are there families in your community whose spouse or parent was killed in the line of duty? Are there single parents who can't afford to move out of gang-dominated neighborhoods? How can you specifically help them? Ask your team to make a list of ways to show the love of God to these victims.

Terrorism

During 9/11, the strength of the United States as a nation was tested as never before. With nearly three thousand lives lost and six thousand more injured in a devastating attack on the Twin Towers, the Pentagon, and the attempted attack on Washington, DC, that same day, we lost a sense of safety and security that has lingered and will continue to linger for decades. But even in the chaos of September 11, 2001, stories of courage arose that kindled our hope for recovery and restoration. The president led the nation in prayer, with many turning to their faith and returning to church to seek answers to their own questions. Even talk-show hosts paused their laughter to call others to pray for victims and their families. What a surreal time that was for our country. Since then so many other countries have also suffered the pain of terrorism.

At a time when a world is in mourning at the senseless and unexpected loss of life, the church is called on to provide a firm foundation for the hurting. Be encouraged by the martyrs of the early church, where Christians were severely persecuted for their faith. Such strength in the midst of persecution or trials should remain an encouragement and an example to the modern church as we stand firm in our faith during times of unspeakable evil.

How should congregations respond to acts of terrorism? While you may feel powerless to help, one of our best tools is prayer. James 5:16 tells us that "the prayer of a righteous person is powerful and effective," so start with prayer. Your team may need to help others in your community cope with feelings of suffering and loss. Many will ask why God let this happen. Consider these four statements about the mystery of suffering from a book by Judith Shelly and Arlene Miller that is often recommended to Christian nurses:

- Suffering came into the world because of sin.
- God is involved in our suffering.
- We can respond to suffering in faith.
- We endure suffering with patience and hope, trusting in God's mercy.[2]

Many world religions embrace suffering because it builds character and draws one closer to God. Charles Stanley shares seven truths about suffering:

1. Adversity is everywhere.
2. Adversity is impartial.
3. Adversity is painful.
4. Sometimes adversity comes suddenly.
5. Times of adversity may be prolonged.
6. Adversity may be intense.
7. Adversity is often beyond our control.[3]

The apostle Paul told us, "but we also glory in our sufferings, because we know that suffering produces perseverance" (Romans 5:3). Likewise, James 1:2 tells us to consider it joy when we have trials because they produce patience and perfect our faith. While these thoughts may not be of comfort to those outside of faith, the comfort that Christians receive from Scripture can be passed on to those who have been hurt by terrorism or similar suffering. A word of caution is needed here. Take care to comfort with grace, humility, and love. Some well-meaning Christians have deeply wounded the hurting using words they thought were encouraging but were in truth judgmental and/or a misuse of Scripture. Colossians 4:6 says, "Let your speech always be with grace, as though seasoned with salt, so that you will know how you should respond to each person" (NASB).

Natural Disasters

Natural disasters occur all around the globe. A good example of the response of the church occurred in 2012. The Church of Jesus Christ of Latter-Day Saints "provided victims of 104 disasters in 52 countries with hundreds of thousands of pounds of food, water, clothing, medical supplies, hygiene kits, and other relief items. In addition, local leaders organized thousands of member volunteers to distribute aid and assist those affected by these disasters, with over 1.3 million volunteer hours of service donated (worth an estimated $28 million)."[4] The church at large in this instance banded together and had a huge impact as they worked with the governments to provide relief.

When expanding your reach, think beyond your own congregation. What is the oversight organization of your church or religion? Do they have a disaster plan to help in times of crises to maximize the church's impact? How can your church participate on a larger scale to help when there are thousands of people affected by natural disasters like hurricanes, floods, tsunamis, tornadoes, earthquakes, or typhoons? The Church of Jesus Christ of Latter-Day Saints has a denominational director of church emergency response. By advance preparation, during Hurricane Sandy, they were able to mobilize about "28,000 church members who donated almost 300,000 hours of service to their communities, working with neighbors to help clean up refuse and debris along the East Coast. Church members also helped to distribute food, water, clothing, cleaning supplies, shovels, generators, water pumps, and other items."[5]

 **Are You Health Aware?**

- How does your congregation interface with the larger church community? Or within your own denomination's leadership?

- What could you do to be part of larger efforts in times of natural disaster? Does your congregation have a plan?

- What does your health ministry team believe about suffering and about helping those who are suffering?

- How do you react to violence in the community? Does your congregation have a plan?

 Health-Aware Checklist

Take an inventory of the following services available in your community and highlight those you feel your health ministry team could make a difference in leading your congregation to greater collaboration and networking.

Community partner	Location/ services	How can we network?
Pregnancy assistance center		
Drug addiction treatment		
Alcoholics Anonymous		
Narcotics Anonymous		
Other types of support groups		
Prison ministry		
Homeless shelters		
Food pantries		
Community recreation center		
Preschools		
Before and after school childcare		
Daycare centers		

Community partner	Location/ services	How can we network?
Hospitals		
Medical centers		
Veterinary clinics		
Local public schools		
Local private schools		
Christian schools		
Child Protective Services		
Adult protective services		
Police and fire stations		
Red Cross		
Salvation Army		

 **Next Steps**

Right now we can:

Within three months, we will:

Our end-of-year goal is:

12

KEEP GROWING A COMPASSIONATE TEAM

"It gave me great joy when some believers came
and testified about your faithfulness to the truth,
telling how you continue to walk in it."
—3 John 1:3

Imagine that your church began its health ministry team three years ago.
The energy behind the start-up was a small group that included June, a
retired community nurse, Paula, a fitness trainer, Anna, a new mother
of twins, and Oliver, an owner of a natural food store. With the support
of the pastor and lay leadership board, the group began their work to
create a safe and healthy environment in the nursery.

In the intervening years, the health ministry, called Wellspring
Inspired, developed an advisory group of twelve members, hosted an an-
nual wellness fair with more than thirty stations, conducted a monthly
blood pressure clinic, supported the advent of three parenting groups and
five fitness groups, and has offered more than twenty classes or pro-
grams on topics ranging from healthy aging to understanding immuni-
zation schedules. Collectively, the congregation has lost more than 650
pounds and made a virtual walk from the church to Jerusalem and back,
just by counting their steps.

While this may sound like the ultimate success story, many chal-
lenges continue to surface. The young adults in the congregation want

more programs focused on topics that interest them, the lay leadership board struggles with the costs associated with the health programing, and they are running out of space for new programs. Wellspring Inspired has never evaluated its programing and process, but they can no longer postpone this important action.

Evaluating your Health Ministry

In addition to evaluating the programs and classes as they are offered, a systematic evaluation of the health ministry as a whole, as it relates to your church's mission, is essential. When an evaluation process is part of a ministry from the beginning, it becomes a natural part of the rhythm of the ministry's work. Ongoing evaluation protects your ministry from becoming forced or punitive. By specifying an annual or biannual review of the actions and processes of the health ministry, the group will benefit from the insights and directives provided by a thoughtful review process.

In creating a quality yet reasonable evaluation process, you will need to think about the design of your evaluation, who will participate, how you will analyze the information collected, what you will do with the information, and how you can improve the evaluation process. As you approach this process, you could ask if any of your members have expertise in designing evaluation tools and processes. A person does not need to be a member of the health ministry team to provide guidance on evaluating the ministry; in fact, it might be best if they are not. If someone has experience in setting up evaluation questionnaires, surveying groups of people, analyzing information, and using this information, then you have found a great resource person who can use their talent to support the needs of the ministry.

When you design your evaluation, you need to think about what questions you will ask and how you will ask them. Are you going to use a paper survey, or will you use an electronic survey sent by email? Will you gather small groups to discuss the health ministry, or will you survey the entire membership? Are you going to use a standard scale for your questions, such as "strongly agree, agree, neutral, disagree, strongly disagree," or open-ended questions, or a combined approach?

It is critical that you capture feedback from participants or stakeholders involved with the programs of your health ministry. A broader inquiry will give you a fuller picture of how well your ministry impacts the lives of those you hope to touch. Do not be afraid to learn from critical comments. Seek to understand all the feedback you receive because the critics may have important insights about how you can improve the ministry.

Who Will Help You Evaluate Your Health Ministry?

- Program participants, church members, and nonmembers
- Nonparticipants
- Critics/skeptics
- Presenters
- Church board members
- Members of the health ministry board
- Clergy
- Community agencies

Once you have gathered information about your health promotion and wellness programs and activities, you will need to organize and analyze the results. Look for consistent themes or areas of agreement. It is natural to focus on negative feedback, but also review where you receive praise. Did your feedback show that your members are interested in longer or shorter sessions? Are there certain groups that are asking for more programing? Are there presenters who stand out as providing useful information? Do your members favor the screening activities of the health ministry? What changes are suggested based on your unique results? It is not uncommon to have additional questions once you get into the results and start looking at how you might use them to strengthen your programs. If that is the case, continue to seek out members and those in the community who can assist you as you move forward.

Evaluation and improvement are part of an ongoing process, so you should also assess what worked well in your evaluation process and be open to figuring out where you could make improvements. Make sure you capture these ideas in your minutes so you can refer back to them when you start the next cycle of evaluation. Those engaged in the current cycle of review may not be part of the group in the coming years. We also know that memory fades over time! It is best to build on your processes of evaluation rather than to start new each time.

Keeping Up with Current Trends

As your health ministry matures, it is important to remain relevant and fresh to the members of your church community. There will be aspects of the program that continue in similar fashion year after year, such as monitoring the safety of the nursery, hosting blood pressure screenings, and/or offering parenting groups. At the same time, are you exploring new topics and areas of interest for your members, such as genetic testing, new fitness apps for the smartphone, tablet, or computer, or examining the latest diet trends? Have you thought about adding a blog to your church website that focuses on wellness?

Ideas for Keeping Up with Trends

- Select journal articles to read and discuss as a group.
- Host a lunch-and-learn, where members bring in hot topics to share.
- Hire a consultant to suggest new directions or trends.
- Attend conferences or presentations (don't forget about webinars).
- Visit another health ministry in your community or where you are traveling for work or pleasure.

- Set up a Facebook group with a focus on sharing program ideas and strategies.

Renewing Your Team

Keeping your team vital and fresh is essential as your health ministry continues in the years ahead. Are you inviting new members to participate not only in programs but also as members of the health and wellness leadership team? An infusion of creative ideas that often comes with the fresh lens of new members could inspire, sustain, or revitalize your health ministry.

In addition to new members, you could offer a one-day retreat for the team with an emphasis on self-care and personal health. There is a tendency for those with caring hearts to give everything they have to others, resulting in a personal depletion of energy and well-being. Consider a day filled with activities like prayer, meditation, connecting with nature, making music, and moving the body as a means to refresh the group and reconnect with one another.

Ways to Renew Your Health Ministry

- Begin meetings with a five-minute devotional about Jesus and his ministry of healing.
- Attend a conference or presentation together.
- Share success stories from your ministry efforts.
- Invite ideas to recharge the energy of the group.

Continuing to Grow

There are many ways that your health ministry can grow. You can expand the number of health promotion and wellness programs you offer. You might measure growth by an increase in the number of participants you serve year by year. You might grow in reputation as a leader in health ministry and help plant the seeds for other faith-based groups. It is important to recognize that, as you grow, your ministry becomes increasingly complex. Do you have the resources, people, space, and finances to continue an upward pattern of growth? As discussed earlier, evaluation is a critical component of a successful program.

It is possible that a health ministry can become too large and perhaps too diverse in its offerings. Continue to monitor your team of providers and the kinds of programs you offer so you are functioning at an optimal level for your church. It is not a competition to see how big you can become. It is always a question of whether your health ministry is providing a meaningful service and making a difference in the lives of your members.

Another way to grow is to grow deeper in relationship with God through the ministry of health and wellness. As John said to his friend Gaius, "Dear friend, I pray that you may enjoy good health and that all may go well with you, even as your soul is getting along well" (3 John 1:2). By creating pathways to health and wellness, you also create an opportunity to minister to others. Your health ministry team and providers should grow in compassion and gentleness as the Spirit of God grows in their hearts. Then they will share not only their knowledge and skills but also the love of God with those receiving assistance through the health ministry.

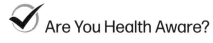

Are You Health Aware?

- What is the biggest challenge about developing an evaluation of your health ministry?

- Is your church familiar with evaluating programs and processes?

- Are you comfortable with the size and reach of your health ministry? What are some ways it could grow?

- What is one way you could renew your health and wellness focus in the church?

Health-Aware Checklist

____ Do you have an evaluation plan for your health ministry?

____ How frequently will you commit to reviewing your program and processes?

____ Do you have anyone with expertise to help create the evaluation plan, or do you need to look for outside resources?

____ Whom will you target to receive the survey and give input on your health ministry? How will you contact them?

____ Who is going to analyze the information you gather, and what will you do with the information?

____ When changes are recommended, how will you implement them?

____ Is your health ministry growing, shrinking, or stagnant?

____ Are members experiencing a deepening in their relationship with God through the health ministry?

____ Are you an open community, inviting new ideas and members to your team?

✅ Next Steps

Right now we can:

Within three months, we will:

Our end-of-year goal is:

NOTES

Chapter 1

1. Brian W. Ward, Jeannine S. Schiller, and Richard A. Goodman, "Multiple Chronic Conditions Among US Adults: A 2012 Update," *Preventing Chronic Disease: Public Health Research, Practice, and Policy*, Centers for Disease Control and Prevention 2014; 11:130389. DOI: http://dx.doi.org/10.5888/pcd11.130389.

Chapter 2

1. Joyce A. Martin, Brady E. Hamilton, Michelle J. K. Osterman, Anne K. Driscoll, and T. J. Mathews, "Births: Final Data for 2015" in *National Vital Statistics Reports*, Volume 66, Number 1 (January 5, 2017).

2. Erik H. Erikson, *Childhood and Society: The Landmark Work on the Social Significance of Childhood, third edition* (New York: W. W. Norton & Company, 1993), 247–51.

3. Ibid., 251–54.

4. Ibid., 255–58.

5. Jean Piaget, *Psychology of the Child* (New York: Basic Books, 1969), 100.

6. Erikson, *Childhood and Society*, 258–61.

7. Ibid., 261–63.

8. National Center for Health Statistics, CDC, "10 Leading Causes of Death by Age Group, United States—2014," National Vital Statistics System, 2014.

9. Erikson, *Childhood and Society*, 263–66.

10. Ibid., 266–68.

11. Ibid., 268–69.

Chapter 7

1. U.S. Office of Personnel Management, Childcare Resources Handbook, https://www.opm.gov/policy-data-oversight/worklife/reference-materials/child-care-resources-handbook/.

Chapter 8

1. U.S. Department of Health and Human Services, Agency for Healthcare Quality and Research, "Women Stay Healthy at Any Age, 2014 Update," Pub. No. 14-IP0002-A.

2. U.S. Department of Health and Human Services, Agency for Healthcare Quality and Research, "Men Stay Healthy at Any Age, 2014 Update," Pub. No. 14-IP0006-A.

3. HHS, "Women Stay Healthy."

4. HHS, "Men Stay Healthy."

5. Office of Disease Prevention and Health Promotion, "2008 Physical Activity Guidelines for Americans Summary," https://health.gov/paguide lines/guidelines/summary.aspx.

6. Katherine M. Flegal, Margaret D. Carroll, Brian K. Kit, and Cynthia L. Ogden, "Prevalence of obesity and trends in the distribution of body mass index among US adults, 1999–2010." *Journal of the American Medical Association* (2012), 307(5):491–97.

Chapter 9

1. National Alliance to End Homelessness in America, "The State of Homelessness in America," https://endhomelessness.org/homeless-ness-in-america/homelessness-statistics/state-of-homelessness-report/.

2. Peter Wagner and Bernadette Rabuy, "Mass Incarceration: The Whole Pie 2017," Prison Policy Initiative, March 14, 2017, https://www.prisonpolicy.org/reports/pie2017.html (article report updated to reflect 2018 numbers).

3. Kairos Prison Ministry International, http://www.kairosprisonmin istry.org/.

Chapter 11

1. ABC News, "Hidden America: Don't Shoot, I Want to Grow Up: Statistics Surrounding Gang Violence in Chicago," 2011, https://abcnews.go.com/Nightline/fullpage/chicago-gang-violence-numbers-17509042.

2. Judith Allen Shelly and Arlene B. Miller, *Called to Care: A Christian Worldview for Nursing*, 2nd ed., rev. and expanded (Downers Grove, IL: InterVarsity Press), 2006.

3. Charles F. Stanley, "7 Truths about Suffering: Understanding the Nature of Our Hardships," InTouch Ministries, November 11, 2016, https://www.intouch.org/read/blog/7-truths-about-suffering.

4. The Church of Jesus Christ of Latter-Day Saints, "Church Responds to More Than 100 Disasters in 2012," *Church News* (March 5, 2013), https://www.lds.org/church/news/church-responds-to-over-100-disasters-in-2012?lang=eng.

5. Ibid.